Zowie!

200+ Ministries Kids Can Do

Jill Goldner   Jodi Blackwell

NEW HOPE
PUBLISHERS

BIRMINGHAM, ALABAMA

New Hope® Publishers
P. O. Box 12065
Birmingham, AL 35202-2065
www.newhopepublishers.com

New Hope Publishers is a division of WMU®.

Library of Congress Cataloging-in-Publication Data

Blackwell, Jodi, 1970-
  Zowie! : 200+ ministries kids can do / Jodi Blackwell and Jill
Goldner.
    p. cm.
  ISBN 978-1-59669-222-0 (sc)
  1. Church work with children. I. Goldner, Jill, 1961- II. Title.
  BV639.C4B53 2008
  253.083--dc22
                                2008009214

ISBN-10: 1-50669-222-7
ISBN-13: 978-1-59669-222-0
N084145 • 0608 • 5M1

Design: Cover designed by Bruce DeRoos, Left Coast Design, www.lcoast.com
Interior: Glynese Northam and illustrator David S. M. Dinkins

"Teaching children to serve and love others through hands-on ministry projects can make a life-long impression on their young hearts. *Zowie!* is a real gem for all parents and workers who are looking for a practical and creative book full of ministry ideas that will teach children to serve others. I can't wait to get this book for all of my children's workers!"

—Diana Duncan, minister of children, Rose Park Baptist Church, Shreveport, Louisiana

"I am always looking for new and creative ideas for our children's ministry. I want our children to know that they have a part in kingdom work. *Zowie!* is a great resource for anyone who works with children and who wants to find unique ways for them to serve others."

—Sally Hearn, minister of childhood education, Temple Baptist Church, Ruston, Louisiana

"Finally, there is a book of fun ideas that challenges kids of all ages and partners with parents as they teach their kids what it looks like to be a Christian in today's world! Thank you, Jill Goldner and Jodi Blackwell, for putting your heads together and coming up with *Zowie!*"

—Kelley James, children's minister, First Baptist Church, Covington, Louisiana

"*Zowie!* offers multiple opportunities to children's leaders. From defining what ministry is, to the easy-to-follow directions for projects, to just the right project to use—according to size of group, cost, and age appropriateness—*Zowie!* is a must-have for ministers who work with kids.

—Cathy Owen, minister of preschool, CrossPoint Church, Trussville, Alabama

"*Zowie!* And that's just what I said after reading this book. Not only does it present over 200 ministry ideas, it also helps leaders teach kids what ministry is and why they minister to others. Organization is a plus to this book. I found activities organized by people's needs, by seasons, and by place. Icons and age-level designations made finding activities a snap. Need to get ready for a mission trip? Help is right here. One word to describe this resource? *Zowie!*"

– Kathy Strawn, coauthor with Beth Moore of *Jesus, the One and Only*

A child is known by his actions. Proverbs 20:11

For my husband, Lloyd.
You are more than words can express, and my love for you grows deeper every day.

And for my incredible daughters, Brook and Autumn.
God shines through you in amazing ways. (P.S. I love you more . . . final!)

—Jodi Blackwell

I would like to dedicate this book to my mom, Ann Jacobs, who continues to teach me the meaning of ministry by setting an example of a humble servant.

—Jill Goldner

Table of Contents

What Can Kids Do?

So, you're ready to do a ministry project with your child or a group of children. That's great! But, before you get started, let's answer some questions you may have.

What is ministry?

What do kids think of when they hear the word *ministry*? Do they picture a man standing at a pulpit on Sunday morning? Maybe they picture a missionary working in a remote part of Africa, Asia, South America, or some city in the Americas. Perhaps they think of a job that requires years of school and training. Your children might be surprised to learn that ministry isn't only for pastors, missionaries, and those with special training. Ministry is for everyone because ministry is about meeting needs. We might define ministry as: serving people in need with the ultimate goal of leading them to a personal relationship with God through His Son, Jesus Christ. This book is a guide to help you lead kids to minister to a multitude of people in a variety of ways.

Why should kids minister to others?

You can't beat the great feeling you get from serving someone in need. You'll see this reflected in testimonials throughout this book, many of which are from participants in the annual Children's Ministry Day™. This special event encourages children to get involved in hands-on ministry. Visit www.childrensmissions.com/childrensministryday.asp.

But as wonderful as serving *feels*, this isn't the main reason children should minister. The best reason for serving others is that God has told us that in serving others, we are serving Him. The Bible says

Love your neighbor as you love yourself.
—Leviticus 19:18

Anyone who is kind to poor people lends to the Lord.
God will reward him for what he has done.
—Proverbs 19:17

In the same way, let your light shine in front of others. Then they will see the good things you do. And they will praise your Father who is in heaven.
—Matthew 5:16

Let us not become tired of doing good. At the right time we will gather a crop if we don't give up. So when we can do good to everyone, let us do it.
—Galatians 6:9–10

Be kind and tender to one another.
—Ephesians 4:32

God is pleased when His people serve others, including children. In His Word, God has provided many examples of people who ministered. The Bible gives examples of young people who served others in unique ways. David ministered to an ailing king by playing soothing music on his harp (1 Samuel 16:14–23). A slave girl ministered to her master Naaman by directing him to Elisha, God's prophet. Naaman was healed of leprosy and learned about the One, True God (2 Kings 5:1–15). The boy king, Josiah, ministered to his people when he chose to serve God instead of idols (2 Kings 22:1–2). Do you remember the boy who came to hear Jesus teach? He ministered by sharing his lunch with 5,000 hungry people (John 6:1–13).

Do you think the biblical record of adults who served also might suggest that God began preparing their hearts during their childhood for the service they would do as adults? In Acts 4:36–37, you can read about Barnabas, the encourager, who once sold property and gave the money to the poor. Acts 8:30–35 tells about Philip, who took time out of his busy day to help an Ethiopian man understand the Bible. In Acts 9:36, you can learn about Dorcas, a woman known for her work with the needy. According to Acts 16:14–15, Lydia, a businesswoman in Philippi, gave Paul and other believers a place to stay during their missionary journey. Acts 18:24–26 tells about a Christian couple, Aquila and Priscilla, who invited a man to their home to teach him about Jesus.

Without a doubt, the best example of a humble servant is Jesus. Acts 10:38 states "Jesus went around doing good." The Gospels tell about the numerous times Jesus healed the sick, fed the hungry, visited with social outcasts, and prayed for sinners. As you read this book, you can learn of ways to help you and your children follow Jesus's example.

To whom should kids minister?

So you're ready to lead your kids in ministry, but you don't know to whom they should minister. Just look around. The world is full of people who are hurting, needy, sick, lonely, and those who do not know Jesus Christ. Here is a list to get you and your children started.

- Residents of a nursing home or veterans' home
- People in assisted living
- Someone who is homebound
- An elderly neighbor
- Patients in a hospital
- Someone in hospice care
- Patients of an AIDS clinic
- A terminally ill neighbor or family member
- Military troops and their families
- Children with special needs and their families
- Prison inmates and their families
- Youth in a detention center
- Homeless people
- Residents of a shelter
- People who have been displaced because of fire or other catastrophes
- Those who require the services of a food pantry or soup kitchen
- Women who need help from a crisis pregnancy center
- Children in foster care
- Sick children
- Needy children in your community
- Children at a local day care
- Community workers and service providers (firefighters, police officers, postal carriers, delivery drivers)
- Migrant workers and their families
- Farmers and their families
- Truck drivers
- Seamen

- Medical care providers (doctors, nurses, dentists, hospital staff)
- People from other cultures living in the community
- International students
- International refugees
- Missionaries and their family members
- Teachers and other school personnel
- Coaches and private instructors
- People on vacation in resort areas

How can you use this book to help kids minister to others?

The Chapters

Once you have decided whom to help, chapters 1 through 3 can help you find a fun and meaningful way for kids to minister. The projects listed in chapter 1 will help you learn how to minister to anyone. Chapter 2 lists a variety of projects that are suitable for ministering to specific people. This will further help you find projects that will be appropriate for the people your children want to serve. The ministry ideas provided in chapter 3 are sorted by season to help you select projects for a particular holiday. Chapter 4 has additional ministry ideas that kids can do at anytime. Check out this list for a number of quick and easy projects. If you would like to take your kids on a mini missions trip, see chapter 5 for checklists, reminders, and other important information that will help organize your outing.

Don't worry if you are still having some difficulty finding the perfect project. The cross-reference index on pages 135–139 will help you to find projects suitable for anyone. Feel free to customize the projects to fit your kids' ministry activities. Many of the projects include hands-on creative work, such as making cards and crafts, which appeals to kids' learning styles. It's important to emphasize to kids the ministry aspect of their creativity. However, the activities in *Zowie!* are not limited to hands-on creativity and crafts; you'll find many other meaningful ministry ideas here.

A special note: Before you embark on a ministry project for a nursing home, day care, or for other similar organizations, contact the organization to make sure the project is suitable for that organization's needs. Accept suggestions and ask if there are any other ways your family or group can help.

The Icons

Under the title of each ministry idea, you'll find a series of icons. Each icon is designed to help you determine at a glance if an idea is right for your child or group. The icons are only suggestions. You may be able to modify each idea to suit your own particular needs.

Ministry Method

The ministry method icons indicate whether a ministry idea is something to make, something to do, something to collect, or someplace to go. Each ministry idea may have more than one icon.

  something to make

 something to do

  something to collect

  someplace to go

Age Level

The age-level icon indicates whether a ministry idea is best suited for preteens (aged 10 to 12). If you do not see this icon, the ministry idea is appropriate for all ages.

Families and Individuals or Groups

The families and individual children icon and group icon indicate whether a ministry idea is for families and individual children or for groups of children. An idea may have one or both icons.

families or individual children

groups

Special Icons

When you see this icon, extra care and adult assistance is necessary. The ministry idea may require the use of an oven, hot-glue gun, sharp object, or other tool that might be dangerous for children.

CAUTION: When you see this icon, special precautions are necessary to ensure the safety of the children.

You'll find one-time, short-term, and long-term ministry projects in *Zowie!*, from craft and cooking projects that will bless others to mini missions trips to prayer journals to performing to sportsathons and so much more. A complete list of **what you'll need** and set of **instructions** come with projects. Project **variations** and **hints** help you to expand project ideas and make them your own. **Sample permissions** and **disclaimers** are available. Please note that while *Zowie!* provides you with the ideas for ministry projects, you gain full responsibility for success as you seek to serve God.

Scattered throughout *Zowie!* are **testimonials** from participants in actual children's ministry projects like those in *Zowie!* that you and your child or group of children will want to try.

Chapter 1

Kids Can Minister to Anyone

Kids of any age can minister to anyone, anywhere. Here are some ideas to get them started.

Write On!

Sometimes the best way to help someone is to pray. Consider starting a family prayer journal. Decorate the journal using the instructions below, or come up with your own idea. Place it in your family room, on the dining room table, or in another area of the house where your family will be reminded to use it daily.

You'll need

black and white composition notebook
adhesive-backed felt or craft foam
scissors
permanent markers
stickers or foam shapes
pen

Instructions

- Cut adhesive-backed foam or felt to the size necessary to cover the notebook.
- Using a permanent marker or foam letters, print the words *Family Prayer Journal* on the front cover.
- Decorate the journal cover with stickers or foam shapes.
- On the first page of the journal divide the page in half by drawing a line from the top to the bottom. At the top of the left side of the page print the words *Prayer Needed*. This is where you will list specific prayer concerns for people you know. At the top of the right side, print the words *Prayer Answered*. This is the place to record when and how the prayer was answered.

Variations

- Instead of adhesive-backed felt or foam, you may wish to use colorful wrapping paper, wallpaper, or adhesive backed plastic to cover the journal. Secure the paper with clear packaging tape.
- You can create pockets in your journal to hold church prayer sheets or other prayer lists. Cut a piece of lightweight cardboard to be 6 inches high and slightly smaller in width than the journal cover. Ask an adult to use a glue gun to attach the edges of the sides and bottom of the pocket to the inside cover.

Testimonial

We began praying about what God wanted us to do and we felt that He wanted us to do something in our own community. We decided to prepare meals at our fellowship hall for some of the people in our community who had fallen on hard times or lost loved ones recently, and some just because we wanted to do something nice for them.
— Loco, Oklahoma

Be Prepared

A great way for kids to prepare their hearts to serve is to focus on Scripture. One of the best ways kids can do this is to memorize Bible verses related to ministry. Begin with Leviticus 19:18, Proverbs 19:17, Galatians 6:9–10, and Ephesians 4:32. To help memorize the verses, kids can:

- Use dry-erase markers to print the Bible verses on a bathroom mirror (with adult permission).
- Use colorful markers to print the Bible verses on note cards. Kids can carry the cards with them wherever they go.
- Print Bible verses on pieces of paper and attach them to a wall. Kids can make paper airplanes and aim the planes at the verses. Kids can earn points every time they hit a target, and then they say the verse.
- Make Bible Verse Catchers. Kids can choose four Bible verses. They can print the Scripture references on the flaps of the catchers and print the Bible verses under the flaps. See instructions below.

Instructions

1. Start with a square piece of paper. Set the paper in front of you so that it looks like a diamond. Fold the right corner to the left corner and crease. Unfold.
2. Fold the bottom corner to the top corner and crease. Unfold.
3. Set the paper so that it looks like a square. Fold it in half horizontally and vertically. Crease and unfold.
4. Fold each corner in to meet the center. Crease.
5. Turn the paper over and repeat step 4.
6. Print a Scripture reference on each triangular flap. Under each flap, print the corresponding Bible verse. Replace the flaps.
7. Fold the square in half so that the printing is on the inside.
8. Kids can decorate the outside flaps as they choose. To make the catcher work, kids can slide their index fingers and thumbs under the outer flaps.

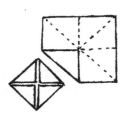

Message in a Bottle

Messages in bottles don't only travel by water. They also travel by postal service. This kid's activity is sure to delight any recipient and capture attention at the post office!

You'll need

a clean and dry plastic water or soda bottle with the bottle lid (remove all wrapping from the bottle)
plain paper (be sure one side of the paper is shorter than your bottle)
markers, pens, or gel pens
paper clips
ribbon or yarn
self-adhesive mailing label (or a piece of paper and clear packing tape)
any fun and appropriate item that will fit into the bottle (see list below)

Instructions

- Print a note of encouragement, a Scripture verse, or any other uplifting message on a piece of paper. For Scripture ideas, refer to the Caring Cards on pages 117 and 118. If you wish, decorate around the message with doodles, drawings, or stickers.
- Tightly roll the paper so that it will slide through the mouth of the bottle. Small hands may need assistance.
- Secure the roll at both ends with paper clips. Then, snugly tie a ribbon or piece of yarn around the special message. Remove the paper clips, and slide the message into the bottle.
- Drop additional items into the bottle to bring a smile to your recipient. You could add: paper confetti (paper punches collected from hole punch trays work great), party confetti (available in the party section of large retail stores and at party supply stores), sequins, small candies, pencils, stickers, small shells, strips of curled curling ribbon, fabric flowers, or anything else your recipient would enjoy. Your items need to be unbreakable, non-perishable, and small enough to fit through the mouth of the bottle.
- When your bottle is ready, tightly screw on the cap and secure with a piece of packing tape.
- Address your mailing label. (If you like, you can add doodles and stickers to the label. Just don't obscure the recipient's address.)
- Attach your label to the bottle.
- Take the bottle to the post office to ensure it gets proper postage.

 CAUTION: A Message In a Bottle could pose a choking hazard to any child under age four.

Variation

Kids can be pen pals with their Message in a Bottle recipients. They can send pictures, stickers, notes, or anything they like. Even more, they can always be ready to tell their pen pal friends about Jesus!

Encouragement Bouquets

Do you know someone who needs encouragement? A kid-crafted paper bouquet blooming with encouraging notes is sure to brighten their day.

You'll need
colorful cardstock (patterned scrapbook cardstock works great)
pencil
scissors
fine-tipped markers
chenille stems
low-temp glue gun (*adult use only*)
floral foam
colorful paper shreds from a crosscut paper shredder or crinkle shreds (available in the gift wrapping section of many retail stores)
small clay pot
decorative ribbon

Instructions
- Lightly draw simple 3-to-4-inch flowers on the cardstock.
- Cut out the flowers and write a note of encouragement on one or more of them. You could write *I care for you*; *God loves you*; or *I'm praying for you*. You might also print a Bible verse. See Caring Cards on pages 117 and 118 for ideas.
- Glue a chenille stem to the back and bottom of each flower. You can cut leaf shapes from cardstock and glue them to the stems.
- Cut a piece of floral foam to fit inside your clay pot. Place some glue in the bottom of the pot and press the foam on top.
- Stick the flowers into the foam in a decorative arrangement. (You may need to cut the stems to shorten them.)
- Place some paper shreds over the foam, and tie a ribbon around the pot. Secure the ribbon with glue.
- A child can deliver the encouragement bouquet with a smile, or even deliver it in secret.

Hint
- Don't be afraid to mix and match papers with different patterns. Choose masculine patterns for male recipients.
- If you use gel glue or tacky glue, allow drying time between steps.

Variations
If you do this activity with a group, simply provide a large flowerpot. Each child can create one flower, and add a note of encouragement.

If you have access to a die cutter with a flower pattern, use die cut flowers. If your flower shape has a hole in the center, cut circles large enough to cover the holes. Kids can write their encouraging notes on the circles and then glue them to the flowers.

B.A.G.S. (Beautiful Acts of Goodness)

Everyone from ages 1 to 101 (or more!) loves to receive a gift. Kids can brighten someone's day by filling a small gift bag with items chosen just for the recipient. A bag might include candy, a bottle of liquid bubbles, small toys, pencils; you name it. Be sure kids include a Caring Card (p. 117–118) or gift tag on each bag.

Ideas for

Teachers and other school staff: A highlighter; a pen (see Pen Pals on p. 62); a thank-you card; candy; or homemade cookies

Friends or other kids: A paper glider or origami art (see Flying God's Love Your Way on p. 72); a Pen Pal (see p. 62); a sponge ball (see Soaked in God's Love on p. 99); candy; a colorful pencil; a mini movie (see p. 65); or a bottle of liquid bubbles

People who are elderly: A card; candy; a package of tissues (see God Bless You on p. 42); origami art (see Wings to Fly on p. 63); or a sun catcher bug (see Bugged! p. 32).

Service people (Police officers, fire fighters, postal carriers) or people in the armed services: A card; candy; a homemade keychain (see Keychain Kindness, p. 73); or homemade cookies.

A child with special needs: An I'm Praying for You Bracelet (p. 66); stickers; a bottle of liquid bubbles; a Wow! Bottle (see p. 87); a sponge ball (see Soaked in God's Love on p. 99); or Teddy Bear Snack Mix (see Jar Mixes on p. 119).

 CAUTION: An adult should supervise the delivery of B.A.G.S. to locations other than schools.

Now You're Cookin'!

Instructions

A great way to minister to others—a family with a new baby, a family going through a crisis, an elderly neighbor, or a teacher—is to make a meal for them. With adult supervision, kids can make a yummy meal that is sure to please even the pickiest eaters.

Check out reputable Web sites to get easy, child-friendly meal ideas and recipes. Good examples are www.pillsbury.com and www.campbellsoup.com. Serve the meal in disposable containers to make it easier for the recipient. Kids can decorate napkins with stickers or make a card to go with the meal. See pages 117-118 for some card suggestions.

Variations

- Instead of making a whole meal, make a simple dessert. The Kraft Foods Web site (www.kraftfoods.com) has good ideas.
- You might also take a small gift to an older sibling.

CAUTION: *This project requires adult supervision. While young children may take part in the food preparation, they should not be permitted to use the stove or oven. Do not permit children to use sharp knives.*

Care Enough to Send Your Very Best

In an age of emails, instant messaging, and text messaging, homemade cards stand out in the crowd. As such, they are a great way for kids to show someone that they truly care.

You can use the following ideas to create cards that are just as fun for kids to make as they are for people to receive. When the cards are finished, kids can personalize them with a brief, heartfelt message expressing their care and God's love. They can even include a Scripture or two. For Scripture ideas, refer to Caring Cards on pages 117 and 118.

Marbleized Cards

You'll Need   white cardstock
9-by-13 baking pan
non-menthol shaving cream
liquid food coloring
plastic forks
piece of sturdy cardboard or large plastic cutting board
broad spatula
paper towels
double-sided tape or glue stick
scissors (plain, pinking, or decorative edge)
fine-tipped markers or pens

Instructions
- Squirt shaving cream into the baking pan until it covers the bottom. Place a few drops of food coloring onto the shaving cream. Use one or several colors. Swirl the color(s) with a plastic fork.
- Carefully place a piece of cardstock on top of the swirled shaving cream. Gently press the paper down. Be sure to press the entire surface of the paper.
- Pull the paper off the shaving cream and lay it on the cutting board, shaving cream side up.
- Hold the paper with one hand and use the spatula to scrape the shaving cream into a trashcan or sink.
- Set the paper aside to dry and begin again.
- When your marbleized papers are dry, cut out rectangles, hearts, flowers, or any shapes. Be sure any shape you cut is smaller than a half piece of paper.
- Fold a clean sheet of cardstock in half. Run a ruler or craft stick along the fold to make it crisp. Glue one or more shapes to the front of the card.
- Use fine-tipped markers or pens to add a special message.

- If you use several colors of food coloring, only slightly swirl them. If you swirl them too much, **Hints** they can quickly become muddy.
- One application of food coloring can provide enough color for two to three prints. When the prints no longer look as you desire, scrape out the used shaving cream and begin again.
- Be sure to wipe the cutting board clean after each use.
- If the paper is wrinkled after it dries, press it between some heavy books.

Purchase blank note cards. Press the front of the cards into the shaving cream. **Variation**

Zoo Who

Kids can decorate cards with a zoo of fingerprint animals.

inkpads **You'll Need**
cardstock
fine-tipped markers

- Fold the cardstock in half, press your fingertip or thumb onto an inkpad, and then onto the cardstock. **Instructions**
- When the prints are dry, use a fine-tipped marker to add ears, legs, snouts, tails, whiskers, horns or anything you choose. Add details such a fingerprint sun or fingerprint flowers. To complete the card, use fine-tipped markers to add an encouraging note and a Scripture verse.

Put a little lotion onto each artist's fingertips. This will help the ink wash off easier. Even so, be **Hint** prepared for some color to linger.

Inkpads work best, but you can also use acrylic paint. Fold a paper towel in half and lay it on a **Variation** disposable plate. Spoon a bit of paint onto the towel, and spread it around. When it's soaked in, press your fingers into the paint and then onto the paper.

You may need to press your finger onto a scrap of paper before making your final print. Experiment, **Hint** and do what works best.

Candy Cards

Children and adults alike will love receiving these sweet greetings. Make them for adults in the hospital, children in the hospital, or foster-care kids. Take some to hand out at a hospital waiting room or veterans' home.

You'll Need   red and green construction paper
scissors
clear tape
flat lollipops wrapped in clear cellophane

Instructions
- Cut a heart shape from red construction paper. The heart should be slightly larger than the top of the lollipop. You can use the heart pattern on page 130 as a guide.
- Use tape to attach the top of the lollipop to the heart. On the other side of the heart print a greeting or Scripture verse (see Caring Cards on pages 117 and 118).
- To make leaves for your lollipop flower, cut two small leaf shapes from green construction paper and tape to the lollipop stick.

Variations   Use a variety of shapes.

- Make a teddy bear-shaped card and tape a lollipop to the bear's paws. Use a gel pen or marker to write a cute message such as *I can't bear it when you aren't feeling well.*
- Make a smiley face cover for a lollipop. Cut two circles from yellow construction paper. The circles should be slightly larger than the lollipop wrapper. Use black marker to make a smiley face on one circle and print a Scripture verse on the other circle. Tape the tops and sides of the circles together, printed sides facing out. Slip the smiley face cover over the lollipop.

Just Popping by to Say Hi

Kids can make these pop-up cards for any occasion.

You'll Need   cardstock
construction paper
markers
scissors
glue
envelope

Instructions
- Copy the pop-up card pattern (p. 124) onto cardstock.
- Cut along the solid lines and fold along the dotted lines.
- Hold the folded paper like a card and be sure the tab you cut is folded inside the card. If you are holding the card correctly, it will look as if there is a notch cut out of the front of the card.
- Cut a shape from construction paper. This is the shape that will pop out when the card is opened. Glue the shape to the folded tab inside of the card as shown in the illustration.
- Use markers to decorate the front of the card. Add a greeting and a Bible verse inside of the card.
- Let the card sit until the glue has dried.
- Fold the card and place it in an envelope.

These cards work best with cardstock. Make the folds crisp by running the edge of a ruler or craft stick along them. **Hint**

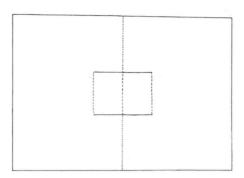

Crepe Paper Cards

For a rainbow of beauty, kids can try this colorful card technique.

You'll Need
crepe paper
cardstock
water
paper towels

Instructions

- Fold the cardstock in half and run a ruler or craft stick along the fold to make it crisp.
- Unfold the card.
- Cut or tear the crepe paper into pieces.
- Place the crepe paper onto one half of the cardstock in any design you choose. Wet a paper towel, wring it out a little, and press it over your design. Leave it in place until it dries.
- Lift the paper towel and crepe paper off the card, revealing a beautiful design.
- Fold the card and write an encouraging message with fine-tipped markers or pens.

Variations

- Cut or tear the crepe paper into shapes to create theme cards. Green or red, orange, yellow, and brown crepe paper can make leaf shapes for spring or fall themes; a rainbow of colors can become flower shapes for spring, Easter, or Mother's Day.
- Place crepe paper on a separate piece of cardstock and dampen as instructed above.
- When dry, remove the paper towel and crepe paper, and then cut the cardstock into shapes and glue the shapes onto your greeting cards. Cut the colored cardstock heart and flower shapes for a Mother's Day card. Use pinking shears to cut the shape of a necktie for a Father's Day card. Cut crosses or eggs and basket shapes for Easter cards. Cut animal shapes to make a card for an animal lover.

Testimonial

We write letters to missionaries at least once a month. They love to hear about the work of the missionaries and they love to receive letters and cards back from them. Out church is small but we have a great amount of ministries going.
— Sacramento, Kentucky

Spin Art Cards

Kids can turn fun spin art into cool cards!

You'll Need   an inexpensive plastic salad spinner (available at large discount retail stores)
cardstock
tape
tempera paint
plain or decorative-edged scissors
fine-tipped markers

Instructions
- Cut a 4-inch-by-6-inch piece of cardstock to fit inside the salad spinner.
- Use a loop of tape to attach another piece of cardstock to the bottom of the spinner.
- Spoon tempera paint onto the bottom of the salad spinner and secure the lid. If the spinner has drain holes in the bottom, set it in a sink or inside a large bowl before adding paint.
- Spin the salad spinner to create paint swirls on the cardstock.
- Fold clean sheets of cardstock in half. Run a ruler or craft stick along the folds to make them crisp.
- Use glue stick to attach the dry spin art to the front of the cards. Trim the edges of the card if you wish.
- Write an encouraging message with fine-tipped markers or pens.

Leaf Print Cards

You'll Need   a variety of fresh leaves
tempera paint
paintbrushes
cardstock
newspaper
white craft paper or copy paper

Instructions
- Fold the cardstock in half. Unfold it.
- Lay a leaf vein-side up on a piece of newspaper and brush tempera paint over the entire leaf. Hold the leaf by its stem if it tries to move.
- Place the leaf on your card, paint side down. Cover the leaf with white paper and firmly rub over the entire leaf. Lift the paper, and peel off the leaf to see your creation.
- When the paint dries, use fine-tipped markers to add an encouraging note or a Scripture verse. See the Caring Cards on pages 117 and 118 for Scripture ideas.

- Make prints with three or more leaves at a time. Use as many colors as you want, but be sure to work quickly so your paint doesn't dry before you make your print. **Variations**
- Set cardstock in a box, lay the leaves on top, load paint onto a toothbrush, and then flick the toothbrush at the cardstock to create a splatter effect.

3-D Cards

Kids can make cards that truly "stand out" in a crowd.

A variety of colorful papers (scrapbook paper, cardstock, wallpaper scraps) **You'll Need**
scissors (plain, pinking shears, or decorative edge)
adhesive foam tape (available in the scrapbook section of craft stores or major retail stores)

- Fold the cardstock in half. Run a ruler or craft stick along the crease to make it crisp. **Instructions**
- Cut a variety of shapes—flowers, airplanes, animals, or anything you like—from the decorative papers.
- Cut small pieces of adhesive foam tape and stick them to the backs of your shapes.
- Remove the paper lining from the foam tape and attach the shapes to the front of your card.
- Use fine-tipped markers or pens to add a special message and Scripture verse to the card.

A Sweet Bouquet

Who doesn't love to get a beautiful bouquet of flowers, especially when they are made of chocolate? Maybe you know someone whose day would be brightened by a bouquet of chocolate roses. These flowers are easy for kids of any age to make.

2 chocolate candy kisses **You'll Need**
5-inch square of red cellophane or pink plastic wrap
green chenille stem
clear tape
green floral tape

- Tape two chocolate candy kisses (still in wrapper) with flat ends together. This will form the rosebud. **Instructions**
- Cover the rosebud with the red cellophane, gathering the edges at one candy point. Twist the cellophane and wrap the end of a green chenille stem around the twist.
- Wrap the area where the stem meets the rosebud with green floral tape.

- Print a Scripture verse on a green construction paper leaf, and use floral tape to attach it to the flower's stem.
- Attach a homemade card to the bouquet.

Balloon Lollipops

Does your child know someone who needs a smile? A new kid in the neighborhood? A child starting kindergarten? A friend who may be sad? An elderly neighbor? A teacher? Kids can help by sending a balloon lollipop.

You'll Need
latex balloons
curling ribbon
12-inch dowel sticks
tape

Instructions
- Blow up a balloon and tie it off.
- Use tape to attach the neck of the balloon to the end of a dowel stick.
- Tie curling ribbon around the base of the balloon and curl it. To curl the ribbon, run it along the cutting edge of a pair of safety scissors. (If you don't have safety scissors, use a hard thin object like a credit card or ruler. Do not use sharp scissors.)
- Punch a hole in the corner of a Caring Card (see pages 117-118). Tie the card to the curling ribbon.
- On the back of the card, write a message welcoming the new child to the neighborhood, the kindergartner to your school, or a note of encouragement to your friend.
- Attach the balloon lollipop to the mailbox or doorknob of your friend or neighbor. It's sure to bring a smile.

Variations
- Turn your gift into a balloon bouquet. Make several balloon lollipops and stick them in a decorated clay pot. See Encouragement Bouquet on page 18 for details.
- Send a card with your balloon bouquet. See the card suggestions on pages 117-118.
- Send a small gift with your bouquet. You could send a Candy Card (p. 21), a candy rocket (see Out of This World! on p. 107), an origami animal (see Wings to Fly on p. 63), or a gift bag (see B.A.G.S. on p. 18).

CAUTION: Balloons are a choking hazard for children under the age of four. Be sure kids caution parents when making balloon creations for very young children.

Bake and Take

There is nothing like homemade baked goods to make people feel welcomed. Choose one of the two recipes provided and make something to take to a newcomer in your neighborhood, someone who is homebound, a new mother, the resident of a veterans' home, or anyone at all.

You'll Need **If you are making pumpkin bread,**

loaf pan
ingredients for pumpkin bread (see recipes on p. 121)
cooking utensils
colored plastic wrap
ribbon
scissors
card
marker

You'll Need **If you are making carrot cake in a jar,**

clean, quart-sized canning jar with lid
ingredients for carrot cake in a jar (see recipes on p. 121)
cooking utensils
fabric square
ribbon
scissors
card
marker

Instructions

- Follow the recipe instructions.
- Make a small greeting card to go with your baked item. See the card suggestions on pages 20–25, 117–118.
- If you made the carrot cake in a jar, cover the top of the jar with a square of pretty fabric and secure with a length of ribbon.
- If you made the pumpkin bread, wrap the loaf in colored plastic wrap. Tie a length of decorative ribbon around the loaf and attach the card to the ribbon.
- Deliver the homemade gift with a smile.

 CAUTION: An adult should supervise the baking and delivery of baked goods.

Testimonial

We are a small country church with just a few children. The children each brought different types of beans which we layered into pint canning jars. We mixed up the spices needed to go with them and gave jars of Patchwork Bean Soup Mix. The church provided a can of stewed tomatoes to go with each jar, which completed everything needed to make the soup. We delivered them to the residents of the Senior Citizens Complex in the town closest to our church, as well as to a few of the kids Grandparents, who are in our church. We delivered 17 jars of soup mix. The kids loved it; it was something they enjoyed putting together and sharing. —Conway, Missouri

Chapter 2

Kids Can Minister to Specific People

The ideas you'll find in this chapter are ministry projects for specific people. You'll find ideas for people who are elderly, sick, in need, at school, from other cultures, in the community, at play, on the missions field, with special needs, and in other situations. Whatever the project, kids can do it!

_____ **People Who are Elderly**

Ideas for ministry to residents of a nursing home, people who are homebound, people in assisted living, residents of a veterans' home, or elderly neighbors

I See a Need

Everyone who wears eyeglasses needs a safe place to put them when not in use. These adorable and easy-to-make eyeglass pouches are sure to please any recipient. Kids can help meet a need as they share God's love with an elderly friend.

You'll Need

sheets of colored craft foam
scissors
small hole punch
plastic lace
plastic pony beads
fine-tipped permanent markers

Instructions

- Cut an 8-by-6-inch piece of craft foam and fold in half so that the 6-inch sides touch.
- Holding the folded piece firmly in your hand, use a hole-punch to make holes around the unfolded side and bottom. The holes should be about ½-inch apart.
- Use plastic lace to sew the pieces together. Begin by knotting the end of the lace. Slip the other end into the first set of holes (back to front).
- Place a bead onto the lace and thread the lace (back to front) through the second set of holes. Pull taut.
- Place another bead onto the lace, and thread the lace through the third hole. Continue until the entire piece has been sewn together. Place a bead on the lace between each hole.
- When you reach the last hole, make a knot.
- Use permanent markers to print a Bible verse and decorate the front of the eyeglass cover.

Hint

Craft foam comes in a variety of colors and patterns. If the glasses case will go to a man, consider using foam that is a masculine pattern or color. Ladies will love the pastel colors available.

Testimonial *The kids at our church gathered cans of soup, colored pre-printed snowman gift bags, and made cards They baked homemade cookies, bagged the cookies, soup, and cards, and delivered these to 19 homes of elderly people in our community. Packages went to both church members and unchurched people in our community.*
— Russellville, Kentucky

Furry Friends

Do you know a child who loves animals? Did you know kids can use their love for animals as a ministry that can touch seniors who are sick, hurting, or lonely? The Delta Society* offers a program where anyone aged 10 and up can learn the skills they and their pets need to safely visit in nursing homes, veteran's homes, and other facilities. The program requires written permission from a parent or guardian, completion of a training course (this can be done either by attending a workshop or by completing a home study course), a health screening of the pet, and an evaluation of the child and his or her pet by a Delta Society evaluator. Once the child and pet pass the evaluation, the child receives an identification badge that lets others know that she or he and their pets are certified Delta Society Pet Partners.

Animals that qualify for Delta Society certification include dogs, cats, guinea pigs, rabbits, rats, goats, horses, potbellied and miniature pigs, chickens, cockatoos, and more.

* For more information about the Delta Society program, go online at www.deltasociety.org or call 425–679–5500.

Note
- To help defray the costs associated with completing the Delta Society program, kids can raise money by having yard sales, bake sales, or penny drives; or, they can write family and friends and ask for sponsorships. Be sure the kids write thank-you notes to each donor.
- Once a child is a certified Delta Society Pet Partner, he or she can create a newsletter of ministry adventures to send to donors, family, and friends.

Adopt-a-Grandparent

Have you ever noticed the way a child can brighten the room with just a smile? Senior adults, especially those in nursing-care facilities, love visits with children, but many don't have grandchildren to visit them. Consider adopting an elderly neighbor, a resident of a nursing home, or someone who is homebound as a grandparent.

To find the name of an elderly person who would benefit from a child's attention, contact a local nursing home or your church office. Children can do many things with and for their adopted grandparents.

- Give a homemade gift of cookies or another yummy treat (see Jar Mixes on p. 119 and recipes on p. 121). Be sure to check for dietary restrictions. **Instructions**
- Do yard work or run errands for your adopted grandparent.
- Collect recyclable items, and take them to a recycling center.
- Send a card or letter.
- Decorate a flowerpot, and give a plant to your grandparent.
- Spend time visiting. Ask questions about what life was like when your grandparent was your age.
- Work on a scrapbook together.
- Find a hobby to do together.
- Read to your grandparent. Read a favorite book or share something you have written.
- Sing or play a musical instrument for your grandparent.
- Offer to take out the trash or feed a pet.
- Take tapes of your Sunday morning worship service to your grandparent.
- Celebrate your grandparent's birthday with a party.
- Offer to help your grandparent decorate for Christmas. Help put the decorations away after the holidays.
- Call your grandparent just to say I love you!

A Cup of Cheer

Kids can brighten someone's day with a tray card or table favor. These clever cards can brighten a dinner tray for a nursing home or veteran's home resident.

cardstock **You'll Need**
scissors
clear tape
tea bags or small packets of instant soup

- Copy the teacup pattern on page 125 onto cardstock. **Instructions**
- Cut out the teacup shape and fold on the dotted lines.
- Tape the tea bag or soup packet to the inside of the card.
- Use markers to decorate the card, and write a greeting on the inside.

Celebrate the Seasons

In many nursing home rooms, a small bulletin board where the resident can display cards and other personal mementos is available. Kids can often brighten a dreary room by putting seasonal decorations on a bulletin board.

You'll Need   construction paper in a variety of colors
scissors
tape or thumbtacks
markers
bulletin board decorative edging (available at office supply and teacher supply stores)

Instructions   Make a seasonal bulletin board display. Use colored construction paper as the background. Add a decorative border and seasonal shapes to the background. For Christmas cut a large tree shape from green construction paper and mount it on a red background. Decorate the tree with colorful ornaments. Print a Bible verse on the tree. In the spring, select a green paper background. Staple or tape silk flowers to the background to look like a garden. For summer you might make a beach scene. Use a blue background for the sky and sea. Add cotton balls for clouds and sandpaper for the sandy shore. Glue beach towels (fabric swatches) to the sand. In the fall attach paper or silk autumn leaves, a cornucopia of fruit, or a turkey to a brown background. All you need is your imagination and a few supplies.

Hint   Over time construction paper can fade. If your bulletin board display will be up for an extended period, you may want to use brightly colored cardstock or scrapbook paper.

Bugged!

Kids can "bug" seniors by making cute sun catcher bugs. When the bugs are hanging and sparkling in windows, they can remind seniors of the children's care and God's creation.

You'll Need   chenille stems (3mm work best)
assorted acrylic crystal jewelry beads
nylon thread
glitter tulle or colorful cellophane
glue
permanent marker
suction cups

Instructions

- Fold a chenille stem in half. Choose two identical beads for the bug's eyes. String one bead onto each end of the stem and slide them to the fold.
- Pinch the chenille stem above the beads and twist. Curl the ends of the stem to make antennae. You now have the bug's head.
- Thread a blunt needle with an 18-inch length of nylon thread. Choose a bead to be the bug's tail and string it onto the thread. Tie it securely. (A teardrop bead like the kind you find on a chandelier makes a great tail.)
- Thread more beads to make the bug's body.
- Cut wing shapes from the glitter tulle or cellophane. Poke the thread through the top of the wings shapes and slide them to the body.
- Attach the head to the body by passing the thread through the space between the fold in the chenille stem and the beads used as eyes. Slide the head to the body. Wrap the thread around the twist above the eyes and tie it.
- If you like, use a permanent marker to add pupils to the bug's eyes.
- Loop and tie the end of the thread around a suction cup.
- Add a Caring Card (see pp. 117-118).
- After kids deliver the bugs, the recipients can hang them in a window and enjoy being "bugged!"

Variations

- Cut two or three sets of wings and thread them onto the bug. The layered effect adds a nice touch.
- Use beads in a variety of colors, shapes, and sizes.

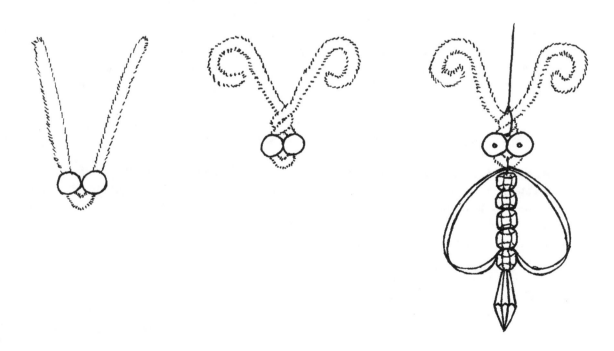

Bone Appetite!

Many senior citizens cherish canine companionship. Showing care to a beloved pets is a great way to show God's love to their owners too. Kids can show their care by making and gift-wrapping some special treats any dog is sure to love.

You'll Need
1 cup all-purpose flour
¾ cup dry milk powder
⅔ cup quick cooking oats (not instant)
½ cup cornmeal
1 teaspoon sugar
½ cup shortening
1 egg
1-tablespoon instant beef or chicken bouillon granules
½ cup hot water
cookie cutters
Gift-wrapping supplies such as paper bags and markers,
cellophane and ribbon, or zipper-topped plastic bags and bows

Instructions
- Add the flour, dry milk, oats, cornmeal, and sugar to a medium-sized bowl. Stir.
- Cut in the shortening until the mixture is blended and crumbly.
- Beat the egg in a small bowl and add it to the mixture. Stir.
- Add the bouillon to the hot water and stir. CAUTION Be sure to let an adult do this step.
- Slowly pour the bouillon broth into the flour mixture a little at a time. Keep adding broth until the dough is moist, but not sticky. (You may not need all of it.) Stir the mixture with a fork until the entire dough is moistened. If the dough is sticky, add a little flour. If it's too dry, add a little water.
- Roll the dough into a ball and knead it on a floured surface for about 5 minutes.
- Divide the dough in half. Roll out each half until it's about ½-inch thick.
- Cut the dough with the cookie cutters.
- Place about six cutouts on a plate and microwave them on medium power for about 4 minutes. Rotate the plate and turn the biscuits over. Microwave an additional 1 to 4 minutes on medium power, checking the biscuits every 30 seconds. The biscuits will be firm or hard to the touch when done. (They will crisp as they cool.)
- When the biscuits are done, cool them on a wire rack.

This recipe makes 2 to 3 dozen biscuits.

Kids can gift wrap the biscuits to add a special touch. They can put them in paper lunch bags decorated with drawings of bones or other doggie themes, wrap them in cellophane that's tied with a ribbon, or seal them in a zipper-topped plastic bag embellished with a bow. Suggest kids add a Caring Card (see pp. 117–118) to the package and deliver it with a smile.

CAUTION: An adult should supervise the baking and delivery of the dog biscuits.

- If you use cookie cutters in a variety of sizes, microwave similar-sized biscuits together.
- Some furry friends have special diets. If possible, check with the owners before making your special treats.

Variations

- Purchase dog treats and package portions to give away.
- When kids deliver the treats to a senior citizen, they can offer to walk his or her dog. Be sure the dog is one the child can control safely. Kids may want to volunteer to walk the dog on a regular basis.

Have Bag, Will Travel

People who use a walker or wheelchair will enjoy having a convenient way to take items with them when they travel. Kids can make this simple sewing craft.

You'll Need

colorful hand towel
two, 24-inch colorful shoelaces (the flat, wide kind) cut in half or ⅝-inch or ⅞-inch grosgrain (GRO-grain) or cotton web ribbon cut into four 12-inch pieces
straight pins
liquid fray prevention (if you use ribbon)
sewing machine (or see hand-stitch and no-sew options below)
Optional: machine washable iron-on patches or appliqués

Instructions

- Lay the towel wrong side up on a flat surface. Pin one end of each ribbon or shoelace strip to each corner of the towel. The ends should overlap the towel about two inches and should be about one inch from the sides of the towel. See illustration.
- Sew the shoelaces or ribbons in place. If you're using ribbon, seal the loose ends with liquid fray prevention and let them dry.
- Fold the towel in half, right sides together. Pin the two sides and sew them together, leaving the end open.
- Turn the towel right side out and voila! You have a bag that can attach to the front of a walker or the back of a wheelchair.
- If you wish, you can decorate the bag with iron-on patches or appliqués.
- Attach Caring Cards (on pages 117 and 118) as gift tags or tuck them inside. Kids can write the words made with love on the backs of the Caring Cards and sign them.

Variations

- If you don't have a sewing machine, you can hand sew this project. Use a sturdy, good quality thread, and tight, even stitches.
- If you don't sew, you can use fabric glue to attach the shoelaces or ribbon and to secure the ends of the towel together.

See illustration on page 36.

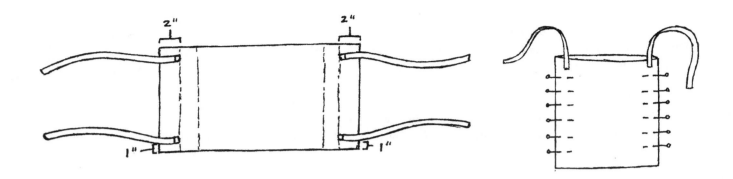

Please Leave a Message

Residents of a nursing home or retirement center love to get visitors, but sometimes they are unable to entertain guests. That's where these mini message centers come in handy. Kids can make door hangers with message clips that will hold notes from visitors.

You'll Need
wooden doorknob hangers (available at craft supply stores)
craft paint
paintbrushes
pre-cut foam or wooden shapes
tacky glue
spring-style wooden clothespins
thin-tipped permanent markers
hot-glue gun
scissors

Instructions
- Kids can paint the wooden doorknob hangers in bright colors. Set the hangers aside and let them dry.
- When the doorknob hangers are completely dry, decorate with foam shapes and markers. Use tacky glue to attach the foam or wooden shapes.
- Ask an adult to use a hot-glue gun to attach a wooden clothespin to the doorknob hanger. This will serve as a message holder.
- Copy Caring Cards on pages 117 and 118. Photocopy and cut out one of the Scripture cards, and clip it with the clothespin.
- Visit with the residents when you take the message holders to the nursing home you have selected.

Variations
- Make magnetic memo holders. Paint spring-style wooden clothespins. Decorate the painted clothespins with buttons or ribbon. Attach a strip of magnetic tape to the back of each clothespin.
- Use pre-cut foam doorknob hangers. Use permanent markers and foam shapes to decorate the hangers.

Our kids did nursing home ministry. Our kids provided fruit, sang songs, helped residents make door hangers for their rooms, and spent time sharing with their new friends.
— Fayetteville, Arkansas.

Testimonial

Underwater Adventure

An aquarium of fish is sure to bring hours of enjoyment to residents of a nursing care facility, veterans' home, or to someone in hospice care.

You'll Need

fish aquarium with pump and filter
fish
gravel
aquarium plants
fish food
small fishnet

Instructions

- Get permission from the director or appropriate staff member of the facility where you would like to set up an aquarium. If agreeable, ask the staff member to help you decide the best place for the aquarium.
- Arrange for only one person at the facility to take care of feeding the fish.
- Check the aquarium weekly to make sure the fish are healthy and the tank is clean and working properly.

Hint

Setting up and maintaining a fish tank can be expensive. Consider asking for donations from a local pet store.

Variation

- Set up a terrarium. It provides greenery without having to be watered.
- Prepare a rock garden outside a window of a common area at a nursing or veterans' home.

Comfort Kits

A senior living alone or in assisted living can become lonely at any moment. Kids can help lessen that loneliness by making Comfort Kits to remind seniors they are loved.

You'll Need	small bottle of liquid bubbles
	cup
	tea bag
	2 chocolate candy kisses with smooth filling
	cloth, foam, or paper heart
	gift bags

Instructions

- Using the pattern on page 130, cut out a heart shape from the cloth, foam, or paper.
- Tuck a small bottle of liquid bubbles, a cup, a tea bag, two chocolate kisses with smooth filling, and the heart into a gift bag.
- Photocopy or hand print the Comfort Kit note on page 127. Use markers to decorate the note with doodles or drawings and tuck it into the bag. Attach a Caring Card (on pp. 117-118) as a gift tag.
- Kids can take time to visit and pray with the seniors when they deliver the Comfort Kits. They can return often to let the seniors know that they truly care. (See Adopt a Grandparent on p. 30 for ideas on how kids can establish a relationship with a senior adult.)

Encore!

Does your child dance or play an instrument? If so, your child can give a recital at a nursing home, veterans' home, assisted living facility, or rehabilitation hospital. One child can give a solo recital or invite friends from church, a dance class, a music class, or a private instructor can come. Contact the volunteer director or recreation director at the nursing home or veterans' home to arrange a time for the visit. Before the big day, encourage children to make programs for the performance. After the recital, kids can stay to visit and pray with the audience.

Testimonial   *"It was very fun to dance for the old people in the nursing home. I liked seeing the smiles on their faces when I danced. It made me feel better."*
                                                                                    —Rebekah, age 8

 CAUTION: If kids go solo, be sure an adult goes along. A group will need at least two adults with them.

Variations

- Kids can take cards or gifts for the audience. They can take Comfort Kits, (p. 37), go Caroling (p. 104), Bugged! bugs (p. 32), Please Leave a Message (p. 36) or other small gifts.
- Take a picture of the performers with each member of the audience. Take the kids back for a return visit to deliver the pictures personally.

Bird Watching

Do you know a senior who enjoys watching birds? A homemade birdfeeder hung outside a window can bring hours of enjoyment to a nursing home resident, homebound person, or hospice patient.

You'll Need

water
¼-ounce package unflavored gelatin
wild birdseed
mini Bundt pans, or another small container with a hole in the center
wax paper
raffia or ribbon
scissors

Instructions

- In a large bowl mix the unflavored gelatin with 2 tablespoons of cold water. Allow to sit for a minute.
- Let an adult add 6 tablespoons of boiling water to the gelatin mixture. Stir 3 minutes or until the gelatin is dissolved.
- Stir 2 cups of birdseed into the gelatin and mix well. Let the mixture sit for a few minutes. Then, stir again. Repeat the process until all the liquid is absorbed.
- Spoon the mixture into the Bundt pans, and place them in the refrigerator for at least 4 hours.
- Remove the bird treats from the molds by turning them over and tapping the bottom of the molds.
- Lay the treats on wax paper and let them air-dry overnight.
- Tie a length of raffia to each bird treat. Leave enough raffia so that the recipient can tie birdfeeders to a tree branch.

Variations

- Gather pictures of regional birds, and make a bird-watching book for the recipient of the feeder. An adult should help kids find pictures on the Internet.
- Make a birdbath using a large terra-cotta flowerpot and a terra-cotta saucer. Turn the flowerpot upside down. Place the saucer on top of the overturned pot. Use clay or a cork to plug the hole in the saucer. Fill the saucer half full of water. Make sure to elevate the birdbath so that it is not too close to the ground.
- Make a birdhouse or another kind of feeder by following directions provided at www.familyfun.com.
- Consider planting flowers or plants outside the window of someone who is homebound.

Pom-pom Pets

Children can brighten the day of someone who receives Meals on Wheels, by making a furry friend to perch on a meal tray.

You'll Need
pom-poms in a variety of colors and sizes
googly eyes
glue
felt
scissors
3-by-5-inch card
marker

Instructions
If your church participates in Meals on Wheels, contact a team member to ask about making these cute tray favors for an upcoming meal delivery. If not, contact the local office that manages meal deliveries. Make cute creatures by gluing pom-poms together. Use brown and tan pom-poms to make a teddy bear or pink ones to make a piglet. Cut small shapes from felt to make ears, noses, and other features. Glue the small features and googly eyes to your creature. Glue each pom-pom pet to a 3-by-5-inch card. Print a message and a Scripture verse on the card (see Caring Cards on pages 117 and 118).

Variations
- Make and deliver a meal to a senior in your neighborhood. See Now You're Cookin' on page 19 for ideas. Include a pom-pom pet with the meal.
- These cute creatures can also be made for hospital or nursing home trays. Or give them to a teacher, friend, or someone who is grieving.

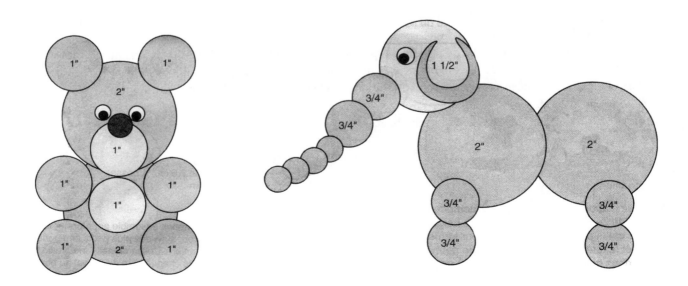

Picking Up the Pieces

Nursing home residents, people who are homebound, and those who are convalescing after surgery will love receiving kid-crafted jigsaw puzzles. The magnetic puzzle pieces will easily stick to a metal tray or cookie sheet.

You'll Need

lightweight cardboard in the size desired for the puzzle
scissors
pencil
markers
adhesive-backed magnets
large envelope
stickers

Instructions

- Kids can use markers to draw a picture, and print a Scripture verse on a sheet of cardboard.
- To create a jigsaw puzzle, turn the picture facedown and draw light pencil lines on the back.
- Divide the cardboard into about 20 pieces.
- Cut along the pencil lines.
- Attach a magnet to the back of each puzzle piece. Place the puzzle pieces in a large envelope.
- Decorate the envelope using markers or stickers.

Variation

Consider donating used jigsaw puzzles to a veteran's hospital or nursing home. Make sure the puzzles have no missing pieces. Ask the administration for permission to set up a small table in a lounge area so that patients/residents and their visitors can gather and work on the puzzles together.

To find additional ideas that are also appropriate for people who are elderly, please refer to the index on page 136.

Testimonial

Our Church prepared homemade vegetable beef soup and corn bread muffins for the elderly shut-ins of our church. ... We delivered a gift bag to each person. We also made cards that included the 23rd Psalm and the signatures of all of our children. We sang and had prayer with these people. [The children] really enjoyed themselves. You could see the joy and delight in the faces of these shut-ins! It was great to be able to share Jesus with the elderly in our community! —Cosby, Tennessee

People Who Are Sick

Ideas for ministry to people in the hospital, sick children, people in hospice care, HIV/AIDS patients, and those who are terminally ill.

God Bless You!

Here is a practical way kids can minister to someone who isn't feeling well. Make paper covers for pocket-sized packages of tissues. Print a verse about God's blessings on the tissue packets (see Caring Cards on pages 117 and 118). Give them to someone who is sick, or, leave them at a funeral home.

You'll Need
cardstock
markers
stickers
scissors
tape

Instructions
- Using cardstock, make the desired number of copies of the tissue cover pattern provided on page 123.
- Use markers and stickers to decorate the tissue covers.
- Cut out the covers by cutting along the solid lines. Be sure to cut out the oval where the tissues are dispensed.
- Fold on the dotted lines, wrapping the cover around a package of tissues. Be sure the tissues can easily come through the dispenser slot. Secure the cover with tape.

Variation
Decorate larger boxes of tissues. Let kids attach stickers to the box and print Scripture verses on clear or white address labels. See Caring Cards on pages 117 and 118 for Scripture ideas. The labels can be attached to every side of the box.

Animal Menagerie

Kids can use this idea to make trays of hospital food a little more enjoyable! (And, in the process, let hospital patients know that they care for them and that God loves them.)

You'll Need
8 ½-by-11 sheets of cardstock cut in half
pencil
scissors

googly eyes   **You'll Need (cont.)**
glue
fine-tipped markers

Instructions

- Fold the cardstock in half. Use a pencil to lightly draw an outline of an animal on the paper. Kids can draw a cat, a dog, a fish, an elephant, or any animal they choose. The only requirement is that some part of the animal (its back, head, tail, and hands) is along the fold. See the animal menagerie templates on page 126 for ideas.
- Hold both layers of paper together and cut along the outline. Be sure to keep some part of the folded side intact.
- Set the animal on a table to be sure it stands up. If the animal does the splits, glue the paper together near the fold.
- Jazz up your animal by adding googly eyes and by drawing a nose, whiskers, stripes, or other details with markers.
- Finally, kids can print the words "God loves you, I'm praying for you, I care about you, and God does, too.", or any other encouraging note on the card.

Busy Bags

It's no fun being sick in the hospital, and it's no fun being stuck in a hospital waiting room either. Children can make busy bags for children who are patients in the hospital or siblings who come for a visit.

Instructions

- Fill a bag, such as a large zipper-topped plastic bag, small fabric tote bag, or paper gift bag with items such as a snack; a small toy; paper, pencils, or crayons; and word games, coloring books, or other activity pages.
- Add a personalized greeting card with a verse.
- Use markers or stickers to decorate the bag.

Laughter Is the Best Medicine

Children can give the gift of laughter by creating joke books.

You'll Need
white paper
construction paper
stapler
markers

Instructions
- Select jokes to put in the joke books. (see p. 122).
- Print each joke on a separate page with the answer written upside down at the bottom of the same page.
- Staple the pages together with a sheet of construction paper for a cover.
- Use markers to decorate the book covers.
- Deliver the joke books to a children's hospital, health clinic, doctor's office, or hospital waiting room.

 CAUTION: An adult should supervise the delivery.

Worth the Wait

When a family is in a hospital waiting room anticipating word about the condition of a loved one, the last thing many people want to do is leave the room to find something to eat. Kids can show God's love in this time of stress by providing waiting room snacks.

You'll Need
individually wrapped snacks
fruit
cookies
candy
bottled water
basket or box

Instructions
- Gather individual packages of snacks such as crackers, peanuts, popcorn, or other crunchy snacks; apples, bananas, or other take-and-eat fruits; homemade cookies or other sweet treats; bottles of water; and a supply of napkins.
- Arrange the snacks in a basket or decorated box.
- Make Caring Cards (pages 117 and 118) and photocopy and punch a hole in the corner of each one. Use a piece of ribbon or yarn to tie cards around the neck of water bottles.
- If possible, take the children with you when you deliver the basket of goodies.

- Pray with the kids of the families you meet. The combination of prayer and care is a powerful ministry.

 CAUTION: An adult should supervise the delivery of the baskets.

Collect quarters to send with the basket. They come in handy when families make trips to vending machines.

Locks of Love

Did you know that girls can use their hair in a ministry? Through a non-profit organization called Locks of Love, girls can donate long hair to be used in making hairpieces for disadvantaged kids suffering from long-term medical hair loss. The main prerequisite for donation is that the hair be in a ponytail or braid that measures at least 10 inches from tip to tip. Also, a parent's permission must be given for a girl to participate in this ministry. To find out more specific information and to learn more about Locks of Love, visit www.locksoflove.org or call 1–888–896–1588. Be sure to follow the specific donation requirements or Locks of Love won't be able to use the donated hair. When people comment about the girl's long hair, she can tell them that she's growing her hair as a gift of God's love for Locks of Love.

Game Peace

Waiting in a hospital or clinic waiting room is certainly no fun and games, especially if a person is waiting for a painful procedure or waiting to hear how a loved one is doing; however, games can help with the long wait.

a collection of board games and card games
coloring books
crayons
basket, plastic storage bin, or book bag
felt-tipped markers
stickers

You'll Need

- Talk to the hospital or clinic volunteer director and explain that you and your kids would like to gather board games, card games, coloring books, and crayons for the waiting room. Ask for advice about which items to donate and where and how to store the items. Allow kids to choose board games that don't have a lot of small pieces (these can get lost easily) and coloring books that depict positive characters.

Instructions

- Kids can attach a Caring Card (see pp. 117–118) to the front of each item they chose.
- Also provide a basket, a plastic storage bin, or a book bag to hold your items. This will keep the items contained and make it easier for staff to keep the waiting room looking nice.
- Kids can even decorate the basket, bin, or bag to make it cheery and colorful.
- Take the games to the waiting room and pray with your kids for the children who will come there. Pray that they will know God's love and experience His peace.

 CAUTION: An adult should supervise the delivery of the items.

Slipper Socks

Skid-proof socks make a great gift for kids in children's hospitals, people in rehabilitation hospitals, and hospice patients. They are also easy for kids to make.

You'll Need dimensional fabric paints
new, thick cotton socks
pieces of cardboard cut to fit inside the socks
ribbon

Instructions
- Slide each sock over a piece of cardboard.
- Squeeze a paint design onto the sole of the sock.
- Allow the design to dry.
- Add designs on top of the sock. Be sure not to add too many designs or the sock may become stiff and uncomfortable to wear.
- When designs are dry, remove the cardboard.
- Use a ribbon to attach a Caring Card (pp. 117–118) to the socks.

Tooth Pillow

Loosing a tooth is an exciting event for a child. But if a child is in the hospital, will the tooth fairy still visit? This simple craft kids can make will allow the tooth fairy to visit, and visit in style!

You'll Need white felt
printed felt
scissors
tacky glue or fabric glue
clothespins or paper clips

- Use the tooth pillow and pocket patterns on page 128 to cut two teeth shapes from white felt and one pocket from printed felt.
- Run a bead of glue along the edge of one felt tooth, leaving about a two-inch gap at the top.
- Place the second tooth on top and gently press the edges.
- Turn your pocket wrong side up and run a bead of glue along the sides and bottom but not at the top. Add the pocket to your tooth.
- When the glue dries, stuff the pillow with fiberfill. You can use a pencil or pen to poke the stuffing into the roots.
- Glue the top closed and use paper clips or clothespins to hold the seam in place while it dries.
- Slide a Caring Card into the pocket and deliver it.

Hint

Printed felt is available in a variety of wonderful patterns: camouflage, tie-dye, cheetah, zebra, alligator, hearts, flowers, sports, and more. Choose a pattern that will work for both boys and girls, or choose two patterns—one for boys and one for girls. If you don't have access to printed felt in your area, solid colors work well, too.

Variation

Kids can collect quarters or dollar bills for hospital staff to stuff in the tooth pillow pockets.

Boo Boo Bunnies

Boo Boo Bunnies are a great way to turn tears into smiles when a child has a minor bump or scratch. They are also easy for kids to make.

You'll Need

lightweight, soft washcloth
rubber band
ribbon
tacky glue
googly eyes
½ or ¾ inch pom-poms

Instructions

- Remove any labels from the washcloth and lay it flat on a table. Tightly roll one corner to the center. Hold this roll in place, and roll the opposite corner to the center as well.
- Keep the washcloth on the table and fold it in half by sliding the two ends together. The tips of the two ends will be the bunny's ears. The fold will be the bunny's body.
- Hold the bunny in the middle, and fold the washcloth in half again, folding the ears up and over the body.
- Wrap a rubber band around the middle of the bunny to make its head. Squeeze some fabric glue under the rubber band at the top and bottom seams. Let the glue dry.
- Tightly tie a ribbon around the bunny's neck. Snip off the rubber band. Add a drop of glue under the ribbon's knot. Glue on the googly eyes and the pom-pom tail.

Tuck a Caring Card (see page 117-118) into your bunny, and deliver to a children's clinic or hospital. The staff can tuck an ice cube or plastic ice cube into the body of the bunny to help soothe minor boo boos. They can also use the bunny as a finger puppet whenever they need an instant puppet show.

Hint Once kids make their first bunny, they can make the rest in the shake of a rabbit's tail.

 CAUTION: Boo Boo Bunnies pose a choking hazard for children under age four. Notify the bunnies' recipients of this hazard. To make the bunnies child-safe, omit the googly eyes and pom-pom tails.

To find additional ideas that are also appropriate for people who are sick, please refer to the index on page 135.

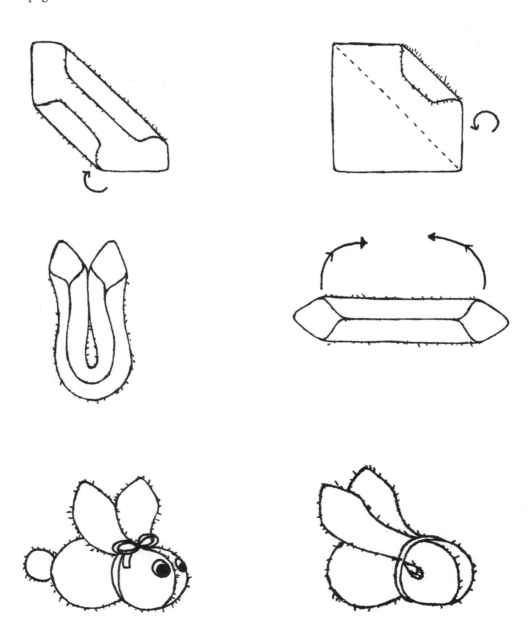

People in Need

The following are children's ministry ideas to help needy families such as people displaced because of fire or catastrophe, homeless people, those who go to soup kitchens and food pantries, residents of women's shelters, residents of family shelters, children in foster care, and women who go to crisis pregnancy centers.

Testimonial

We collected birthday items to make 10 Birthday-In-A-Box kits to donate to Friendship House in New Orleans. Each kit contained items such as cake mix, icing, candles, wrapping paper, blowers, hats, plates, napkins, and small gifts. We delivered the boxes and had a tour of the Friendship House. We heard all about what Friendship House does. It was a fun day for all the kids and leaders.

— Metairie, Louisiana

Verse-a-Day

Do you know someone who is going through a rough time? Maybe the person is sick or grieving or just lonely. A verse-a-day jar is a nice way for children to show they care.

You'll Need

colored paper
scissors
large, clean jar
ribbon
hole punch
3-by-5-inch card
marker

Instructions

- Make a copy of Caring Cards on pages 117 and 118.
- Cut out the verse cards, and place them in a jar.
- Make a card for the front of the jar. For the first line, write Verse-a-Day. For the next line or lines, write Each morning reach into the jar and select a card. Read the verse several times throughout the day.
- Make a small hole in the corner of the card to attach to the jar with a pretty ribbon.

Variations

- Make additional verse cards. Use verses you find in Psalms.
- To make the verse cards prettier, use pinking shears or other decorative edge scissors when cutting them out.
- Mount each verse card on a larger card cut from decorative scrapbook paper or wallpaper scraps.
- Use glass paint or glitter glue to decorate the jar.
- Tape a piece of wrapped candy to the back of each verse card.
- Make a card and write on it Please take one! Use ribbon to hang the card around the neck of the jar.
- With permission, set the jar in a public area of a food pantry, soup kitchen, women's shelter, or another place where people who need encouragement gather.

Paper or Plastic?

Receiving assistance from a food bank or food pantry can be a stressful experience for a family in need. This activity provides kids an opportunity to lessen that stress and brighten someone's day. Before you begin, find out if your local food bank uses paper or plastic bags. Then, choose the corresponding project below.

**For paper
You'll Need**

paper grocery bags
broad-tipped markers
construction paper
scissors (plain, pinking, or decorative edge)
glue sticks

Instructions

- Cut shapes from the construction paper, and glue them to the paper bags. Use the paper shapes to cover any logos or printing on the grocery bag.
- Add additional flourishes with markers.
- Add encouraging notes, Scripture verses (see the Caring Cards on pages 117 and 118 for ideas), or even a joke or two (see p. 122).

**For plastic
You'll Need**

colorful cardstock
scissors (plain, pinking, or decorative edge)
markers
hole punch
yarn or curling ribbon cut into 10 to 12 inch pieces

Instructions

- Cut large, simple shapes— hearts, stars, ovals, squares, triangles—from the cardstock.
- Print an encouraging note, Scripture, or joke on each shape.
- Add flourish by drawing doodles or designs with markers.
- Punch a hole about one-quarter inch from the edge at one end of each shape.
- Loop a piece of yarn or curling ribbon through the hole and securely tie the ends together. Take the completed tags to your food bank, along with a supply of plastic bags. When a food pantry client receives a bag of food, a food pantry volunteer can attach the tag to the bag.

 CAUTION: An adult should supervise the delivery of bags.

Variations

- Make or collect small gifts for children that food pantry volunteers can add to the bags when giving them to clients. You could add: A paper glider or origami art (see Flying God's Love Your Way on p. 72), a Pen Pal (see p. 62), a sponge ball (see Soaked in God's Love on p. 99), candy, a colorful pencil, a mini movie (see p. 65), or a small bottle of liquid bubbles.
- Kids and an adult should go together to deliver the bags. While there, they might be able to volunteer or take part in a tour. Call ahead to make arrangements.

Our area was recently struck by a deadly tornado. Our children worked at a local charity warehouse to sort items that will be given to the victims of the tornado.
— Franklin, Tennessee   **Testimonial**

Stocking Up

Many needy families receive food baskets at Thanksgiving, but what about the other 364 days of the year? Kids can minister to people who don't have enough to eat by starting a food drive. See how many cans and other non-perishable food items your kids can collect.

You'll Need

poster board
markers
large cardboard box
paper grocery bags

Instructions

- Contact your church office, associational office, a local shelter, or community action program to determine if there is a need for food donations.
- Decorate a donation box for collecting donated food. Place the box in your church's foyer or another place where people will see it. Remember to get permission from the proper church staff member.
- Make posters to advertise your canned food drive. Include a goal for the number of cans you would like to collect. Update your posters periodically to indicate new totals of cans collected.
- Call the church office to ask about putting an announcement in the church bulletin or newsletter.
- Ask if you can make an announcement in a worship service.
- Use markers to decorate paper grocery bags. The number of bags will be determined by how many food items you plan to collect. Write a Scripture verse on each bag.
- When your goal is met, place the cans and other non-perishables into the bags you decorated.
- Deliver them to the food pantry you selected.
- Be sure to thank donors for their participation.

Hint

- Items that may be donated include: canned vegetables; canned or instant soups; boxed pasta; cereal; granola bars; macaroni and cheese mix; spaghetti sauce; stuffing mix; instant mashed potatoes; cans or pouches of tuna; vegetable oil; peanut butter; jelly; and crackers.
- When talking with your kids about needy people, avoid stereotypes. Point out that people in poverty are very much like them in other ways. A great resource to read to young children is the book *What Does It Mean to be Poor?* by Joye Smith. Order through www.wmustore.com.

Variations

- Make the food drive a contest between kids and adults. Prepare two donation boxes, one for kids and another for adults.

- Instead of food, collect gently used clothing. Be sure the clothing is clean, current, and in good condition. Donate the items to a local homeless shelter or women's shelter. At the end of the collection period, celebrate by taking the boxes of clothes to a local shelter or placing in your church's clothes closet.
- Pray together for people in your area who are need.

Testimonial *[Children] could choose the project they wanted to do.... One group did homeless ministry through a local church by preparing health kits, creating Bible-verse greeting cards, and decorating for a homeless luncheon. A group did feeding ministry by working through a local food bank. Participants brought healthy snacks and made weekend snack kits for children in our area who need food for the weekend while their parents work. Another group provided a birthday party for a Baptist children's shelter which provides care for children in crisis. Ministry volunteers provided a birthday cake, birthday cards, decorations, and gifts for the residents, as well as lots of fun! Participants also brought non-perishable food items to support two local feeding ministries. We ended our day by gathering for a hot dog lunch and share time.*
— Fayetteville, Arkansas

Care Kits

Going to a homeless or family shelter, entering *foster care, or being displaced by a natural disaster* is a frightening experience for children. Kids can help during this traumatic time by providing Care Kits.

You'll Need a child-sized toothbrush
a tube of toothpaste
soap
shampoo
a washcloth
a hairbrush
activity books
crayons
small toys or games.
sturdy container such as a pencil box, drawstring bag, canvas tote bag, or vinyl gift bag
stickers
felt-tipped markers

Instructions
- Decorate the container with stickers or by drawing designs using felt-tipped markers.
- Package the items in the container.
- Include a Caring Card (see pp. 117-118) with each kit you make.
- Contact your state or local Department of Children's Services before making or delivering Care Kits for children entering foster care.

  CAUTION: Adult supervision is a must if children will help deliver the Care Kits

- In addition to activity books and other items, kids can add a paper glider or origami art (see Flying God's Love Your Way on p. 72), a "Pen Pal" (see p. 62), candy, a colorful pencil, a mini movie (see p. 65), or a bottle of liquid bubbles to the Care Kits. **Variations**
- Kids can make fun soap creations to add to the kits. See Washed in God's Love on page 54.

School Days, School Days

Ahhh, the first day of a new school year! Do you remember standing at the bus stop with a new backpack filled with unsharpened pencils, notebooks with clean white pages, and a brand new box of crayons? Not every parent can afford these things for their child. But kids can help. With adult help, they can organize a school supply give away.

promotional flyers **You'll Need**
cardboard box
school supplies
backpacks

- To begin, create interest and excitement among family members, neighbors, and church family. **Instructions** Make flyers to explain what you want to do and how you plan to do it.
- Ask local stores for school supply donations.
- Ask your church staff to refer you to your associational office or to an agency that can provide a list of children or schools in need of supplies.
- Prepare a donation site. Provide a cardboard box where people can drop off their donations.
- Once you have gathered all the donations, place school supplies into the backpacks.
- Place a Scripture verse inside each backpack.
- With adult supervision, deliver the backpacks.

Bear Each Other's Burdens

Everyone needs a friend, and who doesn't love a cute, furry friend? The gift of a cuddly teddy bear can help a child or anyone who is a child-at-heart feel like someone cares. Kids can start a teddy bear drive. They can give the bears to people who have been displaced from their homes due to a disaster, children in foster care, or others in need of a little attention.

- Make a poster about your teddy bear drive. Tell where you will donate the bears and how many **Instructions** you would like to receive. *Ask for new teddy bears only.*

- Set up a donation center. Decorate the box with teddy bear stickers or pictures. Once you have collected the planned number of bears, use ribbon to tie a Scripture verse tag (see Caring Cards on pages 117 and 118) to each bear's wrist.
- With adult supervision, deliver the bears.

Disaster Relief

Instructions Floods. Fires. Tornadoes. Hurricanes. Terrorism. When disaster strikes, the right help at the right time is critically important. Kids can help in times of crisis by collecting money, toiletry kits, food boxes, cleaning supplies, and other items. Before your children collect any particular item, be sure to check with your local, state, national, or international disaster relief organization to find out what items are needed and where to deliver them. In times of crisis, the wrong kind of help can be the worst kind of help, but the right kind of help can be a gift of hope and healing.

The following organizations provide assistance in times of crisis:
- Disaster Relief (www.NAMB.net)
- The HEART Fund* (www.wmufoundation.com)
  (HEART stands for Humanitarian Emergency Aid for Rebuilding Tomorrow. The HEART Fund collects money to help provide relief for people during sudden disasters and crises.)
- The Salvation Army (www.salvationarmy.org)
- The Red Cross (www.redcross.org)
- Samaritan's Purse (www.samaritanspurse.org)

Variation Some disaster relief agencies collect donations year-round, not just in times of crisis. Check the Web sites of the above organizations to find out more.

Testimonial *Our children made posters and decorated boxes encouraging the church family to donate food items to take to the local food bank. The children unloaded the food, weighed it in, separated it by dry food and cans, marked out the bar codes on the food, and then helped shelve it. The children learned about providing for those less fortunate and learned a little about the process of distributing to the needy. It was a good day!*
— Seguin, Texas

Washed in God's Love

Kids can make these fun and easy soaps to give to kids in need. Whenever the recipients use the soap, they will be washed in God's love.

You'll Need

small plastic animals or toys
clear glycerine microwavable soap (available at craft stores or online)
silicone muffin pan
cellophane
ribbon

Instructions

Place a plastic animal in each cup of a silicone muffin/cupcake pan. Following the package directions, melt a chunk of the soap in a microwave-safe container. Stir the soap to blend any small chunks. Pour the melted soap into the muffin cups. You can cover the animals as much or as little as you like. When the soaps are solid (this will take about an hour), pop them out of the molds. Wrap each soap piece in clear cellophane. Tie the cellophane with ribbon and a Caring Card (see pp. 117-118).

Hint

If you don't have a silicone muffin pan, you can use Styrofoam cups. Coat the insides of the cups with petroleum jelly before you add the soap.

Brother Can You Spare a Blanket?

There is nothing like a warm, cozy blanket on a cold winter night, especially if you live on the street. Kids can organize a blanket drive for a local homeless shelter.

Instructions

- Contact a local homeless shelter and ask about the need for blanket donations.
- Make and display in your church, school, or community colorful posters telling about your blanket drive. Depending on the guidelines of your homeless shelter, ask for new or clean, gently used blankets. Give information about the collection site, your goal, and the deadline for contributions.
- Prepare a donation collection box by decorating a cardboard box.
- With adult supervision, deliver the blankets.

It's a Wrap!

Kids can make no-sew fleece scarves that are sure to keep people warm on even the coldest winter days. They can make these for a homeless shelter, women's shelter, family shelter, or a senior center.

You'll Need

colorful no-sew fleece fabric
ruler
scissors

Instructions

- Cut two 14-by-72-inch lengths of fleece fabric. You may use the same color for both strips or two different colors.
- Place one fleece strip on top of the other.
- Holding the two pieces together, cut a 5-inch square from each corner.
- Time for fringe. Use scissors to make 5-inch cuts at ½-inch intervals all around the scarf.
- Tie each set (back and front) of 5-inch strips together with a double knot. Work all the way around the scarf.

Hint

Look for a variety of patterns and colors of no-sew fleece. Some are designed for guys while other patterns are perfect for women. You can find a variety of kid-friendly patterns as well.

Variations

- To make the scarf more masculine, use dark colors. Also, you can make the tied fringe on the short ends of the scarf only. Since the fleece is no-sew, there is no need to do anything to the long sides of the scarf.
- Organize a winter woolens drive. Instead of making scarves, collect donations of hats, scarves, and gloves. Donate the items to a local shelter.

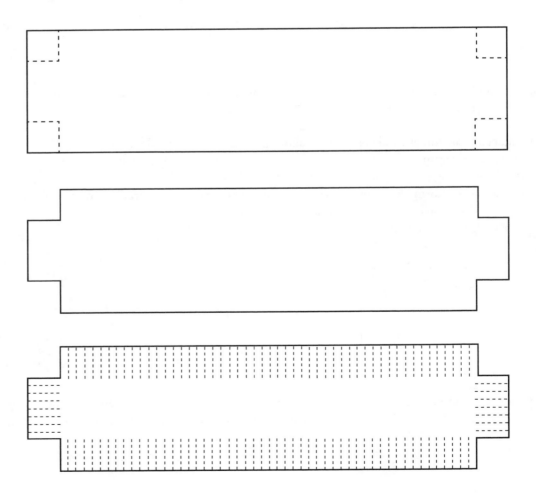

World Hunger Meal

Did you know that of the more than 6.5 billion people in the world:

- 854 million people are hungry
- 1 billion people live on less than $1/day
- 10 million children under age 5 die every year, over half of hunger-related causes. That equals 1 child every 5.4 seconds.
- more than 1 billion people around the world lack clean, safe drinking water

Instructions

Take a day for your family to focus on world hunger. In the morning, wake up and pray for the people in your city, in your state or province, and in your country who will go hungry today. Pray that God would provide the food they need. At night, instead of having a complete meal at supper, serve only rice and water. As you eat, pray for the people in the world who are hungry. Donate the amount of food your family would have eaten to a food bank, or donate a dollar amount for the food you would have eaten to a hunger relief organization.

Testimonial

We started out the day by looking at pictures of families from around the world and at what the families eat each week. After lots of discussion, we bagged up the cans we collected at our church and took off to another church that has a food pantry and ministers to people in the Birmingham area. We learned how the food pantry works and who is eligible. We also saw a short film on poverty. We left the food pantry and went to a grocery store and divided into small groups. Each group planned a week's menu for a family of four and made a grocery list. We went up and down each aisle and priced the items. It was interesting to see how much it costs to eat! —Vestavia Hills, Alabama

> "IF YOU WANT TO BE PERFECT, GO AND SELL EVERYTHING YOU HAVE. GIVE THE MONEY TO THOSE WHO ARE POOR. YOU WILL HAVE TREASURE IN HEAVEN. THEN COME AND FOLLOW ME" (MATTHEW 19:21).

Hint

To find more information on world hunger and how to donate to the World Hunger Fund, go to www.imb.org/worldhunger.

Party in a Box

Do you know a needy family who could use help with a child's birthday party? You and your child can put together a party-in-a-box by placing party items into a decorated shoebox. Take the box to a women's shelter, family shelter, homeless shelter, or family in need.

You'll Need   a shoebox
birthday wrapping paper
clear tape
scissors
markers
birthday party supplies
brightly colored ribbon

Instructions
- Cover a shoebox in birthday wrapping paper.
- Place party items, such as: balloons, birthday paper plates, plastic tablecloth, birthday candles, confetti, party favors, and plastic utensils, into the box.
- Place the lid on the box, and secure by tying a length of ribbon around the box.

Hint   If you use a larger box, you can fit more supplies into the box. Include a boxed cake mix, a bottle of soda, a bag of candy, a wrapped birthday gift, and a birthday card.

Variations
- Prepare a baby-shower-in-a-box for a crisis pregnancy center. Include such items as: pastel-colored paper plates and napkins, a plastic tablecloth, party favors, cake decorations, plastic forks, and small baby items. You may also want to include a party game, such as a list of scrambled baby words. Be sure to include pencils.
- How about a holiday party-in-a-box? Gather items for a Christmas, Easter, or other holiday and place them in a decorated box. Donate the box to a women's shelter or children's hospital.

Testimonial   *Our children collected items to make Birthday Parties in a Bag. We collected items such as spaghetti meat sauce, spaghetti, cake mix, icing, plates, napkins, and decorations. We gathered and made cards and decorated the Birthday Bags and then the children assembled the bags. We assembled 16 bags and took them to a shelter in Shreveport. We were able to meet some residents of the homeless shelter as well have a tour and hear more about the shelter's work.* — Shreveport, Louisiana

The Waiting Game

Spending time in a homeless shelter or women's shelter is often boring for a child. Kids can minister to these children and their parents by making activity books.

You'll Need   activity pages
coloring book pages
construction paper
markers
pencils
stapler

- Gather coloring book pages, word puzzles, and other activity pages. Use several pages for each book.
- Put the activity pages together with staples.
- Make a construction paper cover for each book.
- Use markers and stickers to decorate the booklet covers.
- Remember to print a Scripture verse on each book (see Caring Cards on pages 117 and 118).
- Deliver activity books to a shelter.

Instructions

To make your own puzzles, visit www.puzzlemaker.com.

Hint

Place the activity books with pencils in the waiting room of a doctor's office, dentist's office, or a waiting room of an emergency care unit.

Busy Bags are a great way to minister to families who are traveling by car, train or plane. Include a mini dry-erase board (plastic disposable plate), a dry-erase marker, and tissues. Children can use the boards to draw or keep a running tally of how many different license plates they see. They can also play games such as tic-tac-toe.

Variations

All are Precious in His Sight

Each year thousands of children are placed in foster care. Often all of their worldly possessions are thrown into plastic garbage bags and toted to their new foster homes. Wouldn't it be nice if every child in foster care had a duffel bag or suitcase where they could store their possessions? Kids can help meet that need.

- Contact your state's social services department to determine if there is a need for duffel bags.
- Write a letter asking people to donate new or gently used duffel bags. Explain how the bags will be used. Send the letter to family, friends, neighbors, classmates, and church members.
- Set up a donation collection site. After you have collected several bags, use a permanent marker to print a small message with a Scripture verse inside each bag (see Caring Cards on pages 117 and 118).
- Include a child-friendly translation of the Bible in each bag.

Instructions

- Consider including a teddy bear or small stuffed animal in each bag.
- Provide a Care Kit (see p. 52) for each bag.

Variations

Warm Toes, Warm Heart

For people living on the street, warm socks are a necessity. Kids can help homeless people avoid frostbite, blisters, and other foot ailments by donating socks to a local homeless shelter.

Instructions
- Help kids set a goal for the number of pairs of socks they will collect.
- Guide kids to make posters advertising the sock drive. Place the posters in your church, school, or community.
- Designate a donation site, and provide a box for donations. Kids can use markers to decorate the donation box.
- When the goal is met, deliver the socks to the homeless shelter.

Grab Bags

Often, homeless or hungry people will go to a church for help. If the church doesn't have a food closet, kids can make small snack bags that can be kept at your church office to help hungry people in need.

You'll Need
paper lunch bags
markers
snack items
plastic spoons
napkins

Instructions
- Talk with your pastor or a church staff member to determine if there is a need for these snack bags.
- Decorate the paper lunch bags. Print a Scripture verse on each bag (see Caring Cards on pages 117 and 118).
- To fill the bags, gather items such as: peanut butter crackers, small cans of fruit or applesauce, plastic spoons, juice boxes, cookies, chips, hard candy, granola bars, and small bottles of water. Be sure the items come in individual serving size packages.
- Take the bags to the church office.

Variation
Make a card to put in each bag. See card ideas on pages 117-118.

Host a Reverse Birthday Party

A reverse birthday party is a chance for the person having a birthday to give gifts instead of receive them. Before the party help your child choose a local, national, or international ministry, charity, or other organization to support. On the party invitation the host requests that each guest bring a gift or donation for the chosen organization. The invitations can direct guests to the organization's web site to find a list of needed items, or a list of needed items can be included with the invitation. This ministry not only helps the chosen organization, but also makes a great impact on the guests and their parents too.

Variation

Older children may choose to begin their party at the site of the chosen organization. The birthday child and guests can volunteer their time, and then conclude the party with cake and ice cream at another location. Obtain approval from the organization and find out any special requirements the organization may have for its volunteers. You may also need to obtain permission slips from guests' parents.

 CAUTION: Choose an organization that is in a safe location and that is committed to the safety of its volunteers. Please refer to the safety tips on page 115.

Sponsor a 5K Run

Instructions

Kids can work as a group to sponsor a 5K run for a non-profit organization that supports people in need. With adult help, kids can ask local businesses, radio stations, and churches to sponsor booths and activities. They can help mark the race route and set up sign-in tables and water stations. They can even design a race T-shirt. Most importantly, kids can pray for the event and ask God's blessings over it.

Hint

If possible, secure a park or other property for the route. This avoids the extra logistics and expense involved in using public streets.

Note

In 2004, 10-year old Ellie Ambrose rounded up enough adults to help her start Ellie's Run for Africa. The run raises funds to help African children have better access to education and health care. The run features a 5K run, a 1-mile race for kids, a concert, African dancers, and carnival-like games and activities. Go to elliesrunforafrica.org to learn more about what one child can do.

> "COMMIT TO THE LORD EVERYTHING YOU DO.
> THEN YOUR PLANS WILL SUCCEED" (PROVERBS 16:3).

To find additional ideas that are also appropriate for people in need, please refer to the index on page 140.

People at School

Here are some fun ideas to use in ministry to classmates and friends, teachers, principals, and other school personnel.

Pen Pals

An easy project for any child is covering writing pens with polymer-clay creations. When kids give these special pens to classmates, teachers, and other school personnel, they are showing that they care.

You'll Need   stick pens with an easily removable tip and ink cartridge
polymer clay, such as Sculpey® or Fimo®

Instructions
- Hold the pen by the handle, grasp the writing tip, and pull. The tip and cartridge should come out.
- Now, imagine your pen as a starting point for a clay creation. What could the handle be? A flower stem? A giraffe's neck? Something covered in camouflage?
- Once you have your idea, choose the colors of clay you'll use. Knead the clay until it's soft and smooth.
- Grab a bit of clay in the color your handle will be and roll it into a ⅛-inch coil.
- Begin at one end of the pen and carefully spiral the coil around the handle. You'll want to leave about a -inch gap between each spiral. If your coil runs out before you reach the other end of your pen, just make another coil, and begin the new coil where the first one ends.
- Once the handle is coiled from end to end, gently roll the pen on a clean, flat surface. The coils should flatten and cover the handle in a solid color. If you notice gaps or thin spots, add bits of clay to those spots and roll again.
- Now here's the really fun part. Use more clay to transform the pen into the creation you imagined. Be as creative as you like. Make the features you add smaller than 1 inch to make sure that someone can still hold the pen.
- When the child is finished, ![hand icon] ask an adult to bake the pen according to the clay manufacturer's directions.
- When the pen is cool, snap the ink cartridge back in place. Use string or ribbon to attach a Caring Card (see pp. 117-118) to the creation. Give Pen Pals to a teacher or friend.

Hints

- Wash your hands before changing from one color of clay to another to help your creation look neat.
- Choose designs that a friend or teacher will enjoy.
- Be sure the clay doesn't cover the writing end of the pen: The pen cartridge must go back in place after the clay is bake the clay.
- When adding one piece of clay to another, press it firmly in place to make sure it sticks.

To create a cool swirled effect, make coils in two or three different colors. Stack the coils, twist them together, and then roll them into one coil. Continue as above.

Variation

Survivor: Teacher

Kids can encourage teachers when they give them a fun and inspirational Survival Kits. Children can tuck a plastic cup; a glue stick; a tea bag; a pencil sharpener; a chocolate kiss with smooth filling; a small bottle of liquid bubbles; and a cloth, paper, or foam heart into a gift bag. Use the heart template on page 130 as a guide. Photocopy or hand print the Survival Kit note on page 129. Kids can use markers to decorate the note with doodles or drawings, and then tuck it into the bag, too. Attach a Caring Card (pp. 117-118) as a gift tag.

Wings to Fly

Kids can make mobiles from origami butterflies to let teachers know that they have given the children "wings to fly."

You'll Need

origami paper or colorful paper cut into 8-inch squares
markers, stickers, sequins, glitter, or other colorful materials
pony beads or other acrylic beads
needle and thread
suction cup

Instructions

- Follow the Origami Butterfly instructions on page 134 to make three butterflies.
- Decorate the butterflies with markers, stickers, sequins, glitter, or any other colorful materials. Use thin chenille stems or curling ribbon to add antennae. (Curl the ribbon by pulling it along the dull edge of a pair of safety scissors.)
- Thread a needle with a 36-inch piece of thread. Tie the end of the thread around a pony bead.

- Poke the needle through the center of a butterfly. Slide the butterfly down the string until its belly rests on the bead.
- Add a second bead, and tie it about 3 or 4 inches above the butterfly. Thread another butterfly onto the string.
- Add a third bead 3 or 4 inches above the second butterfly. Thread your butterfly onto the string.
- Remove your needle, and tie the end of the string onto a suction cup.
- Attach a Caring Card to the mobile. On the back of the card, print the words: You have given me wings to fly.

Variations
- Older children can make origami cranes instead of butterflies. Search online or check at your local library to find how to make them.
- Slide the crane onto the end of a pencil or dowel stick.
- Use ribbon to tie a Caring Card around the pencil or dowel.

Memory Book

Just about every teacher loves a heart-felt, homemade gift, and a memory book is one of the best. Kids can ask classmates to write letters or draw pictures for their teachers. Then compile the pictures and letters into an album or scrapbook. Once the book is compiled, they can decorate the cover with felt, fun foam shapes, stickers, or colorful paper. Most importantly, kids can add Scriptures and notes of encouragement throughout the book. See Caring Cards (on pages 117 and 118) for ideas.

Stick Up for Jesus!

Sometimes it is difficult for children to talk to their classmates about Jesus. Here is an easy way for kids to tell what they believe. They can use craft foam to make personalized ministry magnets for school lockers or desks.

You'll Need
pencil
ruler
sheets of craft foam in your school colors
thin-tipped permanent markers
magnets
glue

- Use a pencil and a ruler to draw a pennant shape (large triangle) on a sheet of craft foam in one of your school colors.
- Cut out the triangle.
- Use a permanent marker to write a verse or other message on the pennant.
- You can cut small shapes from craft foam in a different color. Glue the shapes onto the pennant.
- Glue magnets to the back of the pennant.

Variations

- Make more locker or desk magnetic decorations.
- Glue craft sticks in a square to create a frame for your favorite Scripture verse. Attach magnets to the back of the frame.
- Make a mini message holder. Cut a shape from craft foam and glue it to a spring-type clothespin. Attach a strip of magnetic tape to the other side of the clothespin. Print a Scripture verse or message on a small sheet of paper and clip it to the message holder.

Mini Movies

Kids can make their own mini movies to tell friends that God loves them.

You'll Need

white or light colored copier paper
stapler
scissors
pencil
fine-tipped markers
crayons or colored pencils

Instructions

- Stack two or three pieces of paper. Carefully fold the paper in half lengthwise.
- Turn the paper sideways and fold it in half two times.
- Unfold the last two folds, and cut along the fold lines. Tuck these sections into each other to form a book.
- Staple the book along the fold, and then trim the edges to make even. Now you are ready to make your movie.
- On the first page, use a pencil to draw a sad face. Be sure to press hard so that the lines you draw leave an impression on the following page.
- On each page, draw the frown gradually turning into a smile. Make sure each drawing is just a little different from the one before it.
- Once the smile is formed, print the words: Smile, God loves you! on the final page. Or, if there are several pages left, print S on one page, SM on the next page, SMI on the next page, and so on until you have your finished message.
- Preview the movie by holding the book with one hand and using the other to flip the pages from front to back.
- Make any changes you want.

- Trace the drawings with a fine-tipped marker.
- Color the pages, and smile when you give the mini movie to a friend.

Hint The paper along the outside edge of your book should be even. If it isn't, more than one page may flip at once.

Variations
- Draw a basketball player making a slam-dunk, a ballerina dancing, a race car crossing the finish line, or anything you like. Just be sure in your movie to include a note about God or Jesus.
- Use a sticky-note note pad or other small note pad to make the movie. Just add tape to the glued end so the pages of your book won't tear off.

I'm Praying for You Bracelet

Your child can make a bracelet to give to a friend with a promise to pray for that person. The child can make a similar bracelet for herself as a reminder to pray.

You'll Need embroidery floss in 3 different colors
scissors
tape

Instructions
- Cut the embroidery floss into 18-inch lengths. You will need three lengths (each length has six thin strands) for each bracelet.
- Holding the three strands together, make a knot in one end. Tape this knot to a table or other surface.
- Begin braiding the strands together until you reach about two inches from the end of the strands.
- Holding the ends of all three strands together, make a knot about an inch from the ends.
- Remove the tape.
- When you give the bracelet to a friend, help her tie it onto her wrist. Ask her to help you tie the other bracelet to your wrist. Ask your friend what she would like you to pray for. Tell her you will pray for her everyday.

- Instead of making bracelets from embroidery floss, try stringing colorful beads onto a leather cord. **Variations**
- If you will be praying for a boy, make a beaded keychain instead of a bracelet.

Testimonial

We kicked off a partnership with a local elementary school to provide backpacks of nutritious food for children to take home on Friday afternoons in order to provide nutrition on days school meals are not available. Our families met at a local restaurant on Saturday and received a bag and directions for a family scavenger hunt to collect food for these backpacks. They were instructed to have a family time of prayer before setting out on the scavenger hunt. They brought their filled bags to church with them on Sunday.
— Statesboro, Georgia

To find additional ideas that are also appropriate for people at school, please refer to the index on page 135.

People from Other Cultures

These ideas for ministry to internationals, international refugees, international students, and people in other countries and cultures will be great experiences for your child and the recipients.

A Candy a Day

Did you know there are more than 2,200 people groups and about 200 million people who do not have a Bible in their own language? Use the following activity to help groups of kids comprehend this urgent need, and lead them to pray for the many Bibleless peoples of the world.

You'll Need

towel
small zipper-topped plastic bags
one jar filled with approximately 2,200 small candies such as:
jellybeans, hard-coated chocolates, hard-coated chewy candies, or small sour candies (Note: three 16-ounce packages of some brands will provide approximately 3,000 candies.)

Instructions

- Gather kids in a group, and say: *Did you know that there are people in the world who do not have a Bible in their own language? Each piece of candy in this jar represents a group of people who need a Bible in their language.*
- Challenge kids to guess the number of candies in the jar. Then pour the candies onto a towel as you say: Would you believe there are more than 2,200 pieces of candy in this jar?
- Invite each child to take a piece of candy. As the kids eat the candy, lead children to pray for a language group without a Bible to have one soon. Pray for the missionaries who serve Bibleless peoples. Also pray that God will send additional people to minister to the Bibleless peoples of the world.

- Next, give the kids plastic sandwich bags, and invite them to place a handful of candies inside. The kids can take the bags with them, and pray for a Bibleless people each time they take a piece of candy from the bag and eat it.

Hint   If you have extra candies, put them in a hallway or common area of your church or school. The kids can make a sign inviting people who pass by to pray for the Bibleless peoples of the world as they eat the candies. Include a note explaining about the number of Bibleless language groups.

Variations
- Encourage each child to adopt a specific language group for which to pray for. You can find a list of Bibleless people groups, and learn more about Bible translation efforts worldwide at www.wycliffe.org.
- The book *From Akebu to Zapotec: A Book of Bibleless Peoples* is an excellent children's prayer guide. It is available through www.wmustore.com or you can call 1-800-968-7301 to order a copy.

Fruit Label Prayers

instructions   For many people, fruit labels are a necessary annoyance. But have you ever thought of turning them from an annoyance into an opportunity for kids to pray? Here's how. Purchase a world map and place it on a wall. Whenever you or your child peels a label from a piece of fruit, help him locate on the map the country where the fruit is grown. As he attaches the sticker to the appropriate location on the map, pray for that country, its government, for the Christians and missionaries who live there to be bold witnesses for Christ, and for the people who don't know Christ to be ready and willing to receive Him.

Variation   Take this activity further by learning more about your fruit label countries. Find out about each country's geography, culture, and language. If you can, learn a few words in each country's language, and if possible, play a few children's games and make a few foods from your fruit label countries. *Fun Around the World*, and *More fun Around the World*, both by Mary Branson, and *Stirring Up a World of Fun: International Recipes, Wacky Facts & Family Time Ideas* by Nanette Goings are great resources. Refer to page 141 for information.

Kids can also 🔶 ask an adult to help them search the Internet to find information about the fruit label countries; or, find information at the local library.

Oh, for a Thousand Tongues

Does your child know someone her age at school or in your neighborhood who speaks another language? If so, she can spark a friendship by asking the person to teach her the language her friend speaks. As the child learns the language, she can also find out about her new friend's culture. She can learn about the foods, games, and music her friend enjoys, as well as how her friend celebrates birthdays and holidays. As the friendship grows, your child can look for ways to share Christ's love.

 CAUTION: Be sure children to have adult permission and supervision when visiting in homes.

Welcome Home Kit

International college students attending school in the US are far from home. For many, this is the first time they have been away from family and friends. Kids can minister to the international students at a local college in a variety of ways.

Instructions

- To make a welcome kit, begin with a new plastic storage container.
- Fill the container with useful items, such as bath gel, pens, candy, writing paper, stamps, a phone card, quarters, and laundry detergent.
- Make a greeting card to put in each container. See the card suggestions on pages 117-118.
- Collect coupons from local fast food restaurants and stores. Place the coupons in an envelope to include in the welcome kit.
- Kids can look through newspaper inserts and mail circulars to find coupons.
- Invite one or more students to your home for dinner. Kids can help prepare the meal and set the table.
- Kids can make and send greeting cards each month to international students on a campus near your home.

To find additional ideas that are also appropriate for people from other cultures, please refer to the index on page 135.

People in the Community

Use these ideas for ministry to neighbors, delivery drivers, retail workers, day care centers and Head Start programs, police officers, postal workers, firefighters, and other community service providers.

Cookies, Cookies!

Consider baking cookies for your local police station, fire station, or other service station in your community. Choose a favorite family recipe, use the Peanut Butter Kiss Cookies recipe on page 121, or go online to www.pillsbury.com or www.familiyfun.go.com/recipes/kids to find some great, kid-friendly recipe ideas. When the cookies are done, gift wrap them in a decorated paper bag or in a colorful tin. Add a Made with Love gift tag and a Caring Card (pp. 117-118). The Philippians 1:3 Caring Card is a good choice.

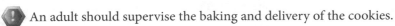 An adult should supervise the baking and delivery of the cookies.

Hint
- Some fire and police stations have to be cautious when receiving home-baked items. Be sure to call ahead and check before taking cookies to someone.
- To help those with food allergies, include a list of ingredients with your gift.

Variation If you have a large group of kids, let each child make and personalize a thank-you card for the people at the service station. See pages 117-118 for homemade card ideas.

Show and Tell

Lights! Camera! Action! Gather the kids in your neighborhood for a puppet show that tells about Jesus. Use the suggestions below to help kids make their own puppets and puppet stage.

You'll Need
paper
pencils
Styrofoam balls
markers
scissors
bandanas or 12-inch squares of fabric
yarn
glue
tension curtain rod

You'll Need (cont.)

sheet
poster board

Instructions

- Get started by writing a puppet script. With a little help kids can write a modern-day story about someone who learns about Jesus from a friend.
- To make puppets, help kids draw faces on Styrofoam balls with markers. They can make hair for the puppets by gluing yarn to the top of the ball.
- Twist scissors into the bottom of each foam ball to create a hole for a finger. Make sure an adult does this step.
- Puppeteers can place a bandana over their hand with their pointer finger extended. Slip the pointer finger into the hole in the puppet's head. They should use their thumb and pinky as the arms for the puppet.
- To make a puppet stage, stretch a tension rod in a doorway. Place a sheet over the rod.
- Make background scenery using poster board and markers.

Hints

- Use a solid Styrofoam ball for the puppet's head. This is a heavier foam ball with a smooth surface. If you can't find this kind of foam ball at your local craft store, use a regular foam ball. Glue foam features to the face instead of using markers.
- If you don't have a tension rod or a doorway to use for the puppet stage, place a sheet or tablecloth over two chairs.

Variation

- Make different kinds of puppets by decorating paper lunch bags with markers, fabric scraps, and yarn.
- Make stick puppets by gluing fabric and yarn to wide craft sticks or wooden spoons.
- Try using your hands and a strong light to make shadow puppets.

Read All About It

Your kids can spread some good news in the community with a good news letter.

With adult supervision, kids can use a computer to design a newsletter. Include community news, puzzles, Scripture verses (see Caring Cards on pages 117 and 118), fun facts, a Bible story, and jokes (see p. 122). Distribute the newsletter to kids in the neighborhood.

Hint

Visit www.puzzlemaker.com for help creating word search puzzles.

Variation

Mail the newsletter to friends in your church or neighborhood.

Flying God's Love Your Way

Looking for a way kids can tell children in the neighborhood God loves them? Let them fold world-record paper gliders* and fly God's love to someone in the neighborhood. Here's how.

You'll Need
8 ½-by-11-inch sheet of paper
flat, firm work surface
markers

Instructions
- Fold the paper in half vertically, like folding your homework (the paper will be long and skinny). Then open up the paper again.
- Turn the paper so that the crease line is perpendicular to the edge of the table.
- Fold the top two corners of the paper towards the centerfold line so that the corners touch about 1 inch from the bottom edge of the paper. You will have a shape similar to a house with a roof.
- Fold up the bottom edge about ¾ of an inch. Repeat 7 times.
- Flip the paper over and fold the glider in half.
- Fold down the top wing about ¾ inch from the centerfold.
- Flip the glider over and repeat the previous step to make the second wing.
- Flip the glider so that the folds are facedown. Make wing tips by folding up the end of each wing at an angle. The wing tip should be about ½ inch tall in the back and should angle to a point at the front (the fold end) of the wing.
- Launch your glider! For best results, throw it straight up and overhand.

See Paper Glider on page 131 for illustrated instructions.

Before kids give their flyers to friends, suggest they use markers to print on the gliders the words: Flying God's love your way; God loves you; or similar messages. They can also use markers to decorate them.

This paper glider once stayed airborne for 27.6 seconds—a Guinness record!

Hint
Use wide-ruled writing pad paper the first time you fold your plane. The lines can serve as guidelines. 1 inch = 2½ lines; ¾ inch = 2 lines

Variations
- Show kids how to fold an origami butterfly, bird, or other shape for a friend. Have them print a message on the paper before they fold it. Then they can tell their friend that there's a secret message hidden inside.
- Instructions for making an origami butterfly are on page 134.
- ! With adult help, search the web for instructions on how to make other simple origami art.
- Make paper gyrocopters. Cut paper into a 7-by-2 inch rectangle. Start at one end, and cut a straight 3-inch slit toward the middle of the rectangle. Fold the two strips in opposite directions. Attach a paper clip to the bottom of the gyrocopter. Hold the gyrocopter above your head and release it to watch it spin.

Keychain Kindness

Habitat for Humanity homeowners are thrilled on home dedication day. The work is finished and the keys to the home become theirs. Kids can add a special touch to this day by creating one-of-a-kind key chains that Habitat staff can give to new homeowners.

You'll Need

one or more colors of polymer clay
rolling pin or clean soft drink can
cookie cutters
key ring

Instructions

- Knead the clay until it is soft and smooth.
- Roll a small portion of clay into a ball. Use a rolling pin or a soft drink can to flatten out the clay. The clay should be ⅛ to ¼-inch thick.
- Cut out a shape with a cookie cutter. Do not use this cookie cutter for food after cutting polymer clay with it. Use additional clay to add designs. Add camouflage splotches, polka dots, flowers, or any design.
- Use a drinking straw to punch a hole at the top edge of the key chain. The hole should be about ⅛-inch from the edge.
- An adult should bake the clay according to the manufacturer's directions.
- When the key chain is cool, thread a key ring through the hole. Use string or ribbon to attach a Caring Card (see pp. 117-118).
- Deliver or mail key rings to a Habitat for Humanity office near you. To find a Habitat affiliate in your area, visit www.habitat.org.

Hints

- Wash your hands before you change from one color of clay to another. This will help keep your creation looking neat.
- If you add one piece of clay to another, press it firmly in place to make sure it sticks.

Variations

- To create a cool swirled effect, make coils in two or three different colors. Stack the coils and twist them together. Fold the coils in half and twist again. Be careful not to over twist or the colors will blend too much. Roll the coils into a ball and continue as above.
- Use a plastic knife to cut out any key chain shape you choose.
- Press clay over hard plastic key chains (the kind used for promotional campaigns) and add clay designs. Contact businesses to see if they have leftover key chains they would be willing to donate.

Let the Games Begin

Often a mother of small children can't get to all the things on her to-do list because of the demands of her children. Kids can create board games to entertain these youngsters in the neighborhood and give moms a break.

You'll Need
poster board or file folder
markers
colorful dot stickers (optional)
game pieces
dice
3-by-5-inch cards
pencil
small plastic zipper-topped bag
candy or small prizes (optional)

Instructions
- Decide on a theme for the game and decide how to design the game board. Possible themes include sports, circus, zoo, hiking trail, and seashore.
- Gather items to use for game pieces. For a circus theme consider using peanuts in the shell [Use caution if a child is allergic to peanuts.] to move from space to space. For a hiking trail theme, use rocks or pinecones as game pieces.
- Print the words Start and Finish at appropriate places on the game board.
- Use colorful dot stickers or markers to create the pathway from start to finish. Decorate the game board to match the chosen theme.
- Make stunt cards for the game with 3-by-5-inch cards. On each card print a silly stunt, such a: hop on one foot while humming a song, or make up a crazy new dance. Each time a player lands on a space of a particular color, they must draw a stunt card.
- Keep game pieces, dice, and cards in a plastic bag for safekeeping. Use candy or small prizes as incentives for winning the game.

Hint
- Instead of creating games, kids can take a few of their favorite board games to entertain neighborhood children. Be sure the games are age-appropriate.

 CAUTION: If you are working with children under three years, don't use game pieces that pose a choking hazard.

This project is not meant to be a babysitting activity, but a way to let a mom get some uninterrupted time to do things around the house. Be sure an adult is nearby.

Walk This Way (Prayerwalk)

Prayerwalking is a powerful way to minister to your community and to the people you see every day. Kids can use the following ideas to do some powerful prayerwalking of their own.

Instructions

- Make a list of your neighbors, friends, and classmates. Pray for each person by name.
- Make a list of the people you see during the week: your teacher, bus driver, coach, mail carrier—anyone at all. Pray for each person by name. Ask God to help each one know His love.
- Make a simple map of your neighborhood. Add names of the people and places you know. Use your fingers to "walk" around the map, and pray for each person and place. Pray that each person would know God's love and that God would use each place for His glory.
- Ask an adult to take you to a neighborhood that is different from your own. Pray for the people and places you see.

Testimony

Our children participated in letter writing to missionaries, children's sermon, and a prayer walk. On a Saturday, we were able to deliver 313 cans of food to a local food bank where our children were allowed to work. We were able to bag over 400 bags of groceries. On Sunday morning, the children led in worship with stories of the projects and singing.
— Marion, Virginia

> "PRAY FOR EVERYONE. ASK GOD TO BLESS THEM. GIVE THANKS FOR THEM" (1 TIMOTHY 2:1).

 CAUTION: Close adult supervision is required for this activity.

Basket of Good Wishes

Kids can welcome a new neighbor to the community with a welcome basket.

You'll Need

a basket or gift bag
a variety of items to fill the basket
greeting card

Here are some items that can be included in the welcome basket:
- cookies or other homemade items (See Recipes on page 121)
- coupons or flyers for local businesses
- menus for restaurants
- flowers

- plant
- tea bags
- coffee

Hint If the family has small children, consider including things like a bottle of liquid bubbles, coloring books, crayons, and candy. Or, make a gift, such as balloon lollipops (p. 26), easy dough (p. 76, below), or mini movies (p. 65).

Read to Me

Preteens can help younger children in your area get a good start in reading by donating books to a local day care and volunteering to read to the children.

Instructions
- Find a local day care or Head Start program that is in need of book donations. Encourage kids to go through their books and make a pile of books that they have outgrown. They can even ask friends, family, and neighbors to donate new or gently used books.
- Have kids make custom bookplates for the books. Print a verse on an address label, and decorate it with markers. Place a bookplate on the inside front cover of each book.
- With adult supervision, deliver the books to the day care or program.
- Encourage kids to volunteer to go to the day care once a week to read to the children.

Variation Kids can make a list of volunteers who would be willing to go to the day care, and read to the children on a regular basis.

Make Some Easy Dough

Kids can follow the simple recipe below to make homemade modeling dough. Children can give a batch to a local day care or Head Start program.

You'll Need 1-cup flour
¼-cup salt
1-tablespoon cream of tartar
1 package unsweetened powdered drink mix
1-cup warm water
2 teaspoons vegetable oil

- In a medium saucepan mix flour, salt, cream of tartar, and powdered drink mix.
- Add oil and water. Mix well.
- Have an adult stir the mixture over medium heat for 3 to 5 minutes or until it forms a ball.
- Remove the dough and knead until smooth.
- Store in an airtight plastic bag or container. Keep in the refrigerator when not in use.

Instructions

Make crazy crayons to donate to a day care or a children's hospital. Collect broken crayons. Remove all paper from the crayon pieces. Place a small handful of crayon pieces in each cup of an old muffin tin. Place the muffin tin into a warm oven, and watch as the crayons melt. When they are soft but not liquid, remove them from the oven, and let them cool. When the crayon mixture hardens, remove from the muffin cups. Place each crazy crayon into a separate plastic bag.

Variation

Adult supervision is strongly recommended when heating modeling dough on the stove or melting crayons for crazy crayons.

Emergency!

Boo boos happen. Every day care center and home with small children can use an emergency first aid kit. Kids can put together first aid kits in containers as they share a special message with the recipients.

a new or sterilized plastic container
markers
bandages and other items for the first aid kit
large adhesive-backed address labels

You'll Need

Print the words First Aid Kit on a large address label attached to the top of the plastic container. Kids can use markers to print verses, such as Psalm 46:1 on additional labels. Attach the labels to the sides of the container. Place first aid items into the container. Here are some items to put in the first aid kit: bandages in a variety of sizes and shapes; gauze; bandage tape; ace bandage; individually-wrapped alcohol wipes; first aid cream; aspirin or pain reliever; rubber gloves; and an ice pack.

Instructions

 CAUTION: Kids should not be permitted to handle any medications. An adult should place pain reliever or first aid cream into the kit.

Balloon Animals

Kids can learn how to make balloon animals and other balloon creations and turn their talent into a ministry.

You'll need   # 260 balloons
hand air pump

Instructions
- With an adult, kids can go online to find instructions for making a balloon dog, giraffe, and bumblebee. Books and kits for making balloon animals available at your local library, bookstore, and at online bookstores.
- Practice, practice, and practice some more.
- Once kids can make balloon creations without a hitch, take the show on the road. Carry a pump and a supply of balloons wherever kids go. When your kids spot children who look sad or lonely, ask for permission to make balloon animals for them.
- When your kids finish the balloons, they can give them to the children, smile, and say, God loves you. They can even hand a Caring Card (see pp. 117-118) to the children or their parents. Kids can spread God's love one balloon at a time.

 CAUTION: Kids should not be allowed to make balloons for someone unless an adult supervises them.

 CAUTION: Some people are allergic to latex balloons.

CAUTION: Balloons are a choking hazard for children under the age of four. Be sure kids caution parents when making balloon creations for very young children.

Hint   Be sure to use a hand pump or ball pump to blow up your balloons. Number 260 balloons are much harder to blow up than regular balloons.

Variations
- Blow up regular balloons and use permanent markers to draw features and faces on them. Add feet to the balloon creations. To make feet, enlarge the heart pattern on page 130. Trace the pattern onto lightweight cardboard, and cut it out. Cut a slit at the point of the heart, and slide the neck of the balloon into the slit.
- Kids can tell a few jokes while they make their balloon creations. Refer to jokes on page 122 for ideas.
- As kids' balloon-making skills grow, they can learn to make more challenging creations.

Scrub-a-Dub

Kids can minister to the members of a group home, senior center, or the community by washing a van or other vehicle.

You'll Need

bucket
soap for washing cars
sponge
hose
soft cloth
trash bag
vacuum (optional)
window cleaner
paper towels

Instructions

Fill the bucket with soapy water, and begin washing the vehicle. Rinse off the soap with the hose. When the whole vehicle has been washed, dry with a soft cloth. Clean out the inside of the vehicle by picking up trash and vacuuming. You may also wash the windows. Leave a small Scripture card on the dashboard (see Caring Cards on pages 117 and 118).

Variation

Consider volunteering to wash windows at a group home, senior center, or the home of an elderly neighbor.

Hint

Have adult supervision when children are washing cars.

Cool Message

Instructions

Have you ever seen sweat pouring off the forehead of the mail carrier as he delivers the mail on a hot summer day? What better way to meet a need than to have a cold bottle of water waiting when he gets to your door?

Using permanent markers, kids can print Scripture verses on adhesive-backed address labels. See Caring Cards on pages 117 and 118 for Scripture ideas. Attach each label to a new bottle of water. Place the bottles in the refrigerator or a cooler with ice. Kids can deliver the bottles with adult supervision.

Variations

- Service providers in the community would love to receive a bottle of cold water. Consider taking bottles of cold water to a local police station, fire station, and town hall. Don't forget store clerks, factory workers, farmers, and construction workers. If there are migrant workers in your area, take a cooler full of water to them where they are working. Kids should always have an adult with them to make deliveries.

- If there is a 5K race in your area, consider giving bottles of water to the participants and on-lookers. Fill a cooler with ice and 8-ounce bottles of water.

Testimonial *There was a prairie fire just outside of our town and we decided we wanted to include an appreciation dinner for our volunteer firefighters. Workers met at the fellowship hall to prepare the meals. Before we began delivering meals, we prayed and read Scripture. We asked God to show people His love through us. We delivered 22 dinners consisting of spaghetti, salad, garlic bread, and cobbler in our community. By 5:00 p.m. we were all back at the fellowship hall preparing for the volunteer firefighters to arrive. At 6:00 p.m., we served 11 firefighters and our 10 workers, along with some of their family members, served a meal consisting of ham, baked beans, potato salad, green salad, white chili, spaghetti (of course!), homemade rolls or garlic bread, and cobbler and cake. We read scripture and the pastor led in prayer before the meal. The firefighters enjoyed the meal so much that the last firefighter didn't leave until 9:00 p.m. God blessed us through this ministry project and we are all anxious to see what our next opportunity to serve God will be.* —Loco, Oklahoma

Markers with a Message

Kids can minister to people traveling through train stations and bus terminals, families vacationing at a resort, people sitting in a hospital waiting room, or anywhere people might be reading a book.

You'll Need
heavy paper
scissors
pen
markers

Instructions Copy bookmarks (p. 124) on cardstock. Print a Scripture verse on each bookmark (see Caring Cards on pages 117 and 118). Decorate the bookmarks using markers or stickers. With permission, leave a stack of bookmarks at a waiting room, train station, or another place where people sit and wait.

Hints
- To make the bookmarks fancier, use scissors with a decorative edge.
- Use rubber stamps and colorful inkpads to decorate the bookmarks.
- Instead of cutting a sheet of cardboard into markers, consider buying blank bookmarks at a local craft store.
- If the church has a ministry for distributing Bibles, kids can place the markers inside the Bibles.

Variation Older kids can print the plan of salvation on bookmarks. Use verses such as: Romans 3:23; Romans 6:23; John 3:16; Ephesians 2:8-9; Romans 5:8; and Romans 10:9-10.

To find additional ideas that are also appropriate for people in the community, please refer to the index on page 135.

People at Play

Use these ideas for ministry with coaches, teammates, and people at community events or on vacation

Go Team!

Kids who play on sports teams can show God's love to teammates and coaches in a variety of ways.

They can

- Arrive early to help set up for practice.
- Stay a few minutes after practice to help put away/load equipment.
- Practice good sportsmanship. Kids can cheer on team members and encourage them whether they win or lose.
- Take a cold bottle of water for each teammate on game days or practice days. Use a string to attach a Caring Card to the neck of each bottle, or write a note to each team member on a label and stick the labels to the bottles. (Be sure to use pens or permanent markers.)
- Host an end-of-the-season party. See Top It Off! on page 98 for ideas.

Not a Last Resort

Many opportunities exist for children to minister at resort locations. Contact the resort minister or chaplain and ask for ways children can help. You'll find some suggestions below.

Kids can

- Pray for the resort ministry staff and volunteers. Kids can also send cards to let the staff and volunteers know they have prayed for them. See the card suggestions on pages 117-118.
- Collect water bottles (see Cool Message on p. 79). Resort ministry staff and volunteers can distribute the bottles to visitors.
- Prepare and donate first aid kits (see Emergency! on p. 77). Kids can place the first aid items in a plastic container or in zipper-topped plastic bags.
- Collect and package travel-sized bottles of sunscreen and bug spray. Seal a set of bottles in a zipper-topped plastic bag and add a Caring Card.
  Note: If you're serving a ski resort, collect sunscreen and lip balm.
- Provide essentials kits for children and adults (see Care Kits p. 52 and On the Road Again on p. 92).
- Collect bandanas for hikers. Attach a Caring Card to each bandana. Or purchase white bandanas and let the kids use a tie-dye kit to decorate them.
- Collect beach balls or Frisbees® for a beach ministry. Kids can use permanent markers to print Bible verses or encouraging notes on the balls or Frisbees®.

- Collect candy, sports equipment, and art supplies for ministry staff and volunteers to use with children.
- Send B.A.G.S. (see pages 79) to summer staff and volunteers at the resort area. Include cards and other items appropriate for the particular resort location.
- Gather Bibles. Resort ministers can give the Bibles to workers, guests, and visitors. Be sure to gather Bibles in other languages, too. Often, international students work at resort locations. Check with your resort minister to discover which languages to gather. Order Bibles in many languages from the International Bible Society. Go to www.ibs.org for ordering information.

Hint   Contact resort ministers or chaplains during the off-season. Remember, when the peak season hits, resort ministers are very busy.

Who Wants a Cookie?

Chocolate chip, peanut butter, or oatmeal? No matter the flavor just about everybody loves a homemade cookie. And that includes race fans. If you live in an area with a NASCAR racetrack, here is a great way for kids to minister to drivers, pit crews, and spectators.

Contact your church or your associational office to find out if there is a cookie ministry at a racetrack in your area. If so, ask about where and when cookies will be collected next. Then, make a batch of homemade cookies for an upcoming race. (See Recipes on p. 121). Place each dozen cookies into a separate large zipper-topped plastic bag. Package the cookies in a plastic container or sturdy shoebox.

If there is no cookie ministry at a track near you, consider starting one. Contact the management office at the racetrack and ask for permission to distribute cookies to the crew members before or after the race. Ask for cookie donations from church members and friends. Give a verse card with each cookie. (See Caring Cards on pages 117 and 118.)

Variation   Kids can help bake cookies for other sporting and community events.

That's Just What I Needed!

Whether it's a fair, a carnival, a parade, a 5K run or any other outdoor event in your community, kids can help. With permission from the event organizers, they can distribute water bottles (see Cool Message, p. 79); sunscreen, lip balm, hand sanitizer, and adhesive bandages; and offer free Bibles or tracts. Before the event, kids can sponsor a drive to collect the needed items. At the site, they can carry baskets or pull wagons containing the items and offer them to staff and visitors.

CAUTION: *Close adult supervision is required for this trip. Each adult should supervise no more than two children. The children should stay with the adult at all times. See the Safety Checklists on page 115.*

To find additional ideas that are also appropriate for people at play, please refer to the index on page 135.

We gathered on Saturday morning to bake cookies and make hot chocolate mix. We also made thank-you notes and appreciation cards. After making these items, we delivered them to one of our local police departments and two of our local fire departments. The children enjoyed doing a service for those who work daily to keep us safe. **Testimonial**

— Conway, South Carolina

People on the Missions Field

These ideas will be fun for children to do as they minister to missionaries and their families.

How can a small yellow fruit help people in other countries hear about Jesus? That's easy! Kids can set up a lemonade stand to raise money for missions efforts around the world.

- Prepare lemonade according to package directions. Add ice. **Instructions**
- Set up a stand by making a poster board sign and attaching it to a table.
- Tell your customers about the project that their money will support.
- When kids are finished selling lemonade, send a check for the total proceeds to the mission organization of your choice (some selected addresses provided on page 141), or the missions organization of your choice.

- Too cold for lemonade? Try making hot chocolate and sell it at school sporting events or holiday **Variations** parades. Be sure to get approval first.
- Not into lemonade or hot chocolate? Encourage kids to start another business and donate the money they make to missions. Kids can mow lawns, weed gardens, wash cars, or lots of other things.

 CAUTION: *The activities above require close adult supervision.*

Miles of Pennies

Youth in North Shelby Baptist Church in Alabama found that, laid side by side, there are about 84,640 pennies in a mile. That is $846.40, and missionaries can do a lot with that much money. Kids can participate in missions efforts around the world by saving their pennies.

You'll Need   plastic containers with lids
scissors
adhesive-backed address labels
markers

Instructions   • Decide where to donate the money collected. Consider agencies or funds such as: World Hunger Fund, World Vision, World Relief, and Wycliffe Bible Translators. Check out WMU new partnerships and programs, such as Pure Water, Pure Love; and other projects of your choice. (See Contact Information on p. 141.)
• Kids can make collection containers by cutting a slot in the lid of a plastic container.
• On an address label, kids should print information about how many pennies they want to collect, where the money will be donated, and what it will be used for. Attach a label to each container.
• Place the collection containers in several places where people will see them and donate their pennies. Be sure to get permission first.
• Empty the containers regularly and keep a running total of the money collected. When you reach your goal, send the money to the agency or fund selected.

Hint   If you don't think you can raise $846.40, consider setting a smaller goal. There are 16 pennies in a foot. Calculate a distance that falls within your range.

Sports-a-Thon

Kids can work with adults and other children to sponsor a Sports-a-Thon to raise money for missions or for a non-profit organization. Children can ask friends and neighbors to sponsor participants for the number of laps they swim; the number of miles they walk, run, or ride; the number of baskets they shoot; the number of hits they make; the number of minutes they jump rope; the number of goals they shoot; or the number of minutes they hopscotch.

After the event, kids can collect the money from their sponsors. Be sure the kids give each sponsor a receipt for his or her donation. Checks can be made directly to the chosen organization.

   CAUTION: Do not permit children to go out alone to solicit and collect money from sponsors. They should have adult supervision at all times.

Party!

Have a party with a purpose. Kids can minister to their friends and missionaries when they host an international party to raise awareness about missions efforts around the world.

Instructions

- Plan the food and activities for the party. For refreshments serve tortilla chips and salsa (Mexico). Let the guests try using chopsticks (China) to eat their chips. Use paper fans and lanterns (Japan), flags from different countries, and a world map for decorations. Plan to have a piñata (Mexico) and play hopscotch (many countries) and jackstones (Kenya). Jackstones is played like jacks, but using almonds instead of metal jacks.
- Send out invitations. Consider writing the information on pieces of a world map.
- Contact the International Mission Board (www.imb.org) to learn ways to pray for missionaries in countries all over the world.
- Print missionary names or prayer requests on paper fans for kids to take home as party favors.

Hint

For more ideas of international foods, games and crafts, check out www.gapassport.com or www.childrensmissions.com.

Variation

Older kids can host a World Crafts party for their friends. World Crafts is a nonprofit organization that imports handmade items from countries around the world. When people purchase these handcrafted items, they help to support the families of artisans around the world who live in poverty. To learn more about World Crafts, visit the Web site: www.worldcraftsvillage.com.

Mission Possible

Millions of people in many different countries haven't heard the good news of Jesus. But, you might be thinking, what can kids do? How can they help reach lost people around the world? Here are some practical things kids can do to support missionaries at home and around the world.

Instructions

- With adult supervision, kids can visit missions Web sites, for example, the North American Mission Board Web site. Select a missionary for whom the child would like to pray. After praying, send an email saying, "I prayed for you today."
- Kids can save their allowance and purchase a missions DVD and invite friends over for a movie night. Don't forget the popcorn!
- Start a missions club in your community. Contact, for example, the International Mission Board to obtain copies of the Kids on Mission newsletter and other resources.
- Read a missionary biography. Read about Paul's missionary journeys in the Book of Acts. As you read, make a list of ways someone might have helped the missionary. Commit to help a present-day missionary by doing one of the things on the list.

- Obtain a copy of the a missionary prayer calendar. Each week, pray for the missionary children who have birthdays that week.
- Call a missions prayerline every week for a month. (See page 141 for some toll-free phone numbers.) Write down prayer requests and put them under your pillow. Pray for them when you go to bed at night or when you awake in the morning.
- Pray for a different unreached people group every night for a month. To learn more about the many unreached people groups around the world, visit www.childreninaction.com, www., the International Mission Board Web site: www.imb.org, or www.praykids.com.
- Pray for a Bibleless people group every night for a month. To learn more about Bibleless peoples, visit the Wycliffe Bible Translators Web site at www.wycliffe.org. See A Candy a Day (p. 67) for additional information.

To find additional ideas that are also appropriate for people on the missions field, please refer to the index on page 135.

People with Special Needs

Here are some ideas to minister to people with special needs.

Be a Friend

Kids can show God's love to children with special needs. Kids can pray for their friends with special needs, spend time with them (invite them over, eat lunch with them, play with them), send them cards or notes in the mail, go to the movies together, or invite them to church. The possibilities are endless!

Bubbles!

Completing daily tasks can be difficult for the parents of a special needs child. Older kids can minister to these parents by offering to entertain their child for an hour or two.

You'll Need   a bottle of liquid bubbles
assorted bubble wands
books
squirt guns and other toys for water play
towels

Interview the parent of a special needs child to find out what kinds of activities the child enjoys. Be sure to ask about restrictions. Most children like making bubbles and playing in water. Make a list of the activities to do with the child. Gather the necessary supplies. Plan to spend an hour or two. **Instructions**

Some children are afraid of water. Be sensitive to the child's fears. **Note**

 CAUTION: *Adult supervision is a must for this project.*

In addition to bubble and water play, consider looking at books, doing simple puzzles, playing finger games, playing with a ball, playing with sand, or dancing to music. **Variation**

Wow! Bottles

Movement and color fascinate many children with special needs. Kids can fill water bottles with a variety of objects to create toys that will capture the interest of a child with special needs.

empty water bottle (clean and dry, with the wrapper removed) **You'll Need**
small magnetic objects such as colorful paper clips or small magnetic letters
rice or play sand
glitter
funnel
plastic tape
jumbo craft stick
button magnet
low-temp hot glue gun

- Pour rice or sand into the water bottle until the bottle is about ⅔ full. Add some glitter. A funnel will help. **Instructions**
- Drop the small magnetic objects into the bottle.
- ⬡ An adult can run a bead of hot glue around the threads of the bottle. Quickly screw on the lid.
- When the glue cools, wrap some plastic tape around the lid to ensure the seal.
- Shake the bottle to distribute the objects.
- Use hot glue to attach a button magnet to the end of a craft stick.
- Print a Bible verse or encouraging note on the back of the craft stick. See Caring Cards on pages 117 and 118 for ideas.

The child with special needs can use the magnetic stick to move the objects inside the bottle.

Our children collected non-perishable food, sorted the food, and we distributed half of the food to a **Testimonial**
local mission that helps those in need in our community; they hold weekly Bible studies, services and Sunday meals. When someone needs food, they can go here and get it. We donated (and stocked our church's food pantry with the other half of the food. Our church provides food for those who come to

our church and need help. Our group was very blessed in this opportunity to serve those in need. It was a wonderful experience for us all.
— Livingston, Tennessee

Hint   If you use rice, make it colorful. Pour rubbing alcohol into a bowl, add food coloring, and stir. Add rice and stir. Pour the rice into a strainer and then spread it onto paper towels. When the rice is completely dry, continue as above.

Variations
- Fill the bottle ¼ full with light corn syrup or mineral oil. Add water until the bottle is ¾ full. Add food coloring and glitter. Secure the lid as above.
- Fill the bottle ¾ full with water. Add crayon shavings. You can make shavings by sharpening crayons in a hand-held pencil sharpener. Secure the lid as above.

Learning Is the Key

Children can have many kinds of special needs such as autism, cerebral palsy, Downs syndrome, hearing impairment, sight impairment, spina bifida, or Sensory Processing Disorder. One of the best ways kids can minister to a child with special needs is to learn about the particular disability the child has. With adult help, kids can search the Internet to learn about the disability. Then, they can use the ideas in this section or search the other ministry projects in this book to find ones that will help them minister to the child.

Hold It!

To help someone with limited dexterity hold playing cards without dropping them, kids can make this simple and easy cardholder.

You'll Need   2 large plastic can lids
ice pick or utility knife ADULT USE ONLY
metal paper fastener
tape
colorful stickers

Instructions   Hold the lids together with the smooth sides facing, and punch or cut a small slit in the center. Stick a fastener through the hole and splay the ends. Cover the splayed end with tape. Decorate the holder with stickers, and use permanent markers to add Scriptures or encouraging notes.
   Players can slide their cards between the lids to hold them while they play their favorite game.

Kids can give a deck of cards or a card game with each holder. They can even play a game with the recipient. **Variation**

You Said It!

One way children can minister to people who are hearing impaired is to take time to learn American Sign Language. With adult help, kids can search online to find a web site that teaches American Sign Language. Children can also find excellent sign language books at many local libraries. Who knows? God might use a child's knowledge of sign language to show His love to people who are hearing impaired.

Does your child know someone her age who is hearing impaired? She can ask her friend to teach her sign language. **Variation**

Other People

Here are some ideas for ministry to military personnel, seamen, migrant workers, truck drivers, prison inmates, and youth in a detention center:

I Care Packages

Whether they are stationed overseas or living at a local military base, soldiers love to receive care packages. Is there someone in your family, church, or community who serves in the military? A great way kids can show their support for that person is to prepare a care package.

You'll Need
shoeboxes
items to put in the boxes
markers
brown paper
clear tape
scissors
paper

Instructions
• Collect items for military care packages. You can include: hot chocolate packets; writing paper; pens; stamps; puzzle books; books; phone cards; sunscreen; lip balm; soap; toothpaste; shaving gel; nail clippers; batteries; pre-moistened hand wipes; hand sanitizer; playing cards; and magazines.

- Place the items you have collected into a shoebox. Include a Scripture card (see Caring Cards on pages 117 and 118) and a personal greeting in each box.
- Wrap the boxes in brown paper and decorate with markers.
- Address and mail the package(s). If you don't have a specific soldier in mind, contact a local military recruitment office for suggestions on where and how to send the care packages.

 CAUTION: Children should not include last names or personal information when writing notes for the care packages.

Highest Honors

Kids can honor the men and women who risk their lives for their country. Here are a few ideas to consider.

Instructions
- Take a plant and visit with a patient at a veterans' retirement home.
- Make cookies and take them to a military base. Call for permission first.
- Make greeting cards for the patients at a veterans' hospital. (See card ideas on pp. 117-118.)
- Clean up a veterans' cemetery or war memorial in your town. Pick up trash and rake leaves.
- Write a thank-you note to a soldier.
- Send a care package to a soldier on active duty. (See Care Kits on p. 52.)

The Comforts of Home

Men and women who work on cargo ships are often away from home for months at a time. If you live in an area near a seaport, kids can minister to these seamen.

Instructions
- If your association participates in a port ministry, contact your associational office to get information about items needed and how to distribute goody bags. Otherwise, contact the local port authority to ask about this ministry project.
- Collect items for each bag. Items may include: hot chocolate or drink mix packets; writing paper; pens; stamps; puzzle books; books; phone cards; sunscreen; lip balm; soap; toothpaste; toothbrush; deodorant; shampoo; shaving gel; nail clippers; batteries; pre-moistened hand wipes; hand sanitizer; playing cards; and magazines. You may also want to include a homemade baked item. (See Recipes on p. 121.)
- Place several items into a bag. Kids can make a greeting card with Scripture verse for each bag (see Caring Cards on pages 117 and 118 and card suggestions/ideas on pp. 20-25).
- With adult supervision, deliver the goody bags to the designated site.

Variations

- Don't live near a seaport? Perhaps you live in a farming area where migrant workers come to help during harvesting season. A migrant worker might also benefit from a bag of goodies. Contact your church staff or associational office to learn about ongoing ministries to migrant workers in your area.
- You can also donate bags to people who have been displaced from their homes due to disaster.
- These goody bags would also be a welcome treat for college freshmen away from home for the first time.

 CAUTION: Personal contact between seamen and children should be supervised and kept to a minimum. Never share personal information, including last names.

Gotta Keep Rollin'

A truck driver's life on the road is no piece of cake. But with this cute and simple tractor-trailer craft that kids can make, it can be a few pieces of candy.

You'll Need

15-piece packs of gum
individually wrapped, square fruit chew candies
Sweet and sour hard candy pieces
low-temp hot glue gun Adult use only
glue stick

Instructions

- Have an adult put a drop of glue on a fruit chew candy. Stack another fruit chew on top. Line up the edges and press the candies together.
- When the glue cools, turn the candies so they look like books on a bookshelf. This is the cab of the truck. Use more glue to attach the cab to the end of a pack of gum. This will be the trailer. Let dry.
- Cut and glue small pieces of aluminum foil or gum wrapper foil to the cab for windows. If you wish, add white hole punch headlights, too.
- Glue a Caring Card to the side of the trailer where the writing is upside down. Finally, an adult should hot glue 10 Sweet Tart wheels to your rig: two to the cab and eight to the trailer (four at the front and four at the back). The Caring Cards are larger than 1 ¼-by 2 ¾-inches so you will want to photocopy and reduce the cards to fit the side of the package of gum.

 CAUTION: An adult should supervise the delivery of the candies. Personal contact between truckers and children should be kept to a minimum. Caution children to never share personal information, including their last names.

Variations

- Make tanker trucks. Instead of using a 15-piece pack of gum, an adult can hot glue a roll of Life Savers onto a 5-piece pack of gum. Make the rest of the truck as described above. Use string or yarn to attach a Caring Card.
- Give a candy rig to a farmer in your community. They're on the road a lot, too!

On the Road Again

Kids can help keep the truck drivers in your area by collecting items for essentials kits. They can collect toothbrushes; travel-sized soap, shampoo, and shaving cream; disposable razors; washcloths; bandages; and gum, mints, or other candies. Kids can seal each set of items and a Caring Card (see pp. 117-118) in a zipper-topped bag.

Hint   Be sure to collect soaps, shampoos, razors, and shaving creams appropriate for men and women too.

 CAUTION: An adult should supervise the delivery of the essentials kits. Personal contact between truckers and children should be kept to a minimum. Caution children to never share personal information, including their last names.

Variations
- Kids can also make candy tractor-trailer rigs (see Gotta Keep Rollin on p. 91) and add them to the kits.
- Deliver some Bone Appetite bags (see p. 34) with your essentials kits. For many truck drivers, canine companions are part of the family.
- Kids can make essentials kits for migrant workers, prison inmates at a local jail, or youth at a detention center. If you make the kits for prison inmates or youth at a detention center, check for restrictions first!

Happy Birthday!

Is there a detention center for youth in your area? If so, consider contacting the chaplain or volunteer director and offering your family or group to have a birthday party for one of the youth.

Instructions
- Ask for any restrictions or special instructions.
- Kids and adults should work together to bake and decorate a cake (if possible, find out the youth's favorite kind).
- Make cards (see the card suggestions on pp. 19-25).
- Gather party hats, balloons, and other decorations.
- Write a special message in a Bible and gift-wrap it.
- As you prepare, pray that the person having a birthday will know God's love and care in a special way.

If birthday parties are not permitted, ask the chaplain to suggest another way your family or group can minister to a youth on his or her birthday. **Hint**

 CAUTION: *Personal contact between youth and children should be highly supervised. Caution children to never share personal information, including their last name.*

Something as simple as a birthday cake can move a youth at a detention center to tears. One youth said, "Nobody's ever given me a birthday cake before!" Quoted in I Can Do That! *by Cathy Butler.*

We met at the church first. Then we divided into groups. One group went shopping for everything needed for a birthday party (they put together two parties): cake mix, cake pan, frosting, candles, balloons, etc. The other group bought "kids comfort foods" (foods that they themselves like to find in the pantry and that can be easily prepared by kids). These kids bought things like pop tarts, cookies, popcorn, drinks, etc. We then returned to the church and packed the items in bags we had previously decorated for this event. After that we went to the area shelter for victims of domestic violence. We got a tour of the facility and also met (with her permission) a current resident and her 6- year-old daughter. We spent time playing with this young girl outside on the shelter's playground. After we returned to the church the girls almost unanimously voted that playing with the little girl was the best part of the day and that shopping for her made them feel important. She put a human face on what we were trying to accomplish. Also, each girl had made a Tee-shirt at our meeting earlier to wear. The staff and people that we met commented on our colorful shirts and we were able to share with others about Children's Ministry Day and what we were doing to provide Hope to the Hungry. Thanks for letting us be part of the great works and in spreading the love of Christ! **Testimonial**

— Shallotte, North Carolina

Chapter 3

Kids Can Minister in Any Season

During holidays and special seasons, children can use these ideas for ministry.

_____ Spring

Tis the Season

During the Christmas season lights and decorations fill most neighborhoods, but what about at Easter? Share an important message with your neighbors as you create an Easter lawn display.

    Suggest that children plan an Easter lawn display. They can make posters, create an Easter story handout to place in a basket, or decorate a large cardboard box to show scenes from the Easter story. Begin by reading together the story of Jesus's death and resurrection (Matthew 26:1 – 28:20).

Instructions

Make a Thanksgiving lawn display. Include posters about being thankful. In large block letters write out verses, such as Psalm 136:1 and Psalm 118:28-29 on poster board.

Variation

A Basket of Cheer

Kids can minister to children who are sick by putting Easter baskets together and delivering them to a children's hospital.

baskets
decorative grass
plastic eggs
candy
small toys
construction paper
markers
ribbon

You'll Need

Instructions   Kids can fill plastic eggs with candy and small toys. Using construction paper and markers, they can make an Easter card to put in each basket. Or they can use one of the card suggestions on pages 117-118. Be sure to include Scripture verses that tell about Jesus's death and resurrection. (See Matthew 26:1–28:20.) Tie a colorful ribbon to the handle of each basket. Kids and adults should go together to deliver baskets to a children's hospital.

Variation   Kids in homeless shelters or women's shelters would be thrilled to receive an Easter basket. Call a shelter in your area to determine if there is a need. Ask where you can donate the baskets.

 CAUTION: Some children in the hospital may have diet restrictions. Check with medical staff before giving a basket of candy to a child. You may want to prepare non-food baskets for children who can't have goodies.

Egg Hunt

All children like Easter egg hunts, but how can you minister with a basketful of plastic Easter eggs? Kids can organize and host an egg hunt in their own backyards.

You'll Need   plastic Easter eggs
candy
slips of paper
pen
paper lunch bags
markers

Instructions
- Read about Jesus's death and resurrection in Matthew 26:1–28:20.
- Print meaningful verses from the death and resurrection story on individual slips of paper.
- Place the slips of paper and candy into the plastic eggs.
- Decorate bags for kids to use as they collect the Easter eggs.
- Hide the eggs around the backyard.
- Invite kids from the community to the egg hunt.
- Help the kids read the verses hidden in their eggs.

Make a Mother's Day

Mother's Day can be a stressful time for a mother living in a women's shelter, family shelter, or correctional facility. Kids can brighten her day by creating Mother's Day cards just for her. Use card ideas from pages 20-25, or use children's ideas. When the cards are finished, kids can use fine-tipped markers to print the words *Happy Mother's Day from someone who cares for you—me* on the inside of the cards.

Variations

- Kids can create a special Mother's Day Encouragement Bouquet (p. 18) for the shelter or correctional facility.
- If possible, visit a family shelter with your kids, and let the kids play games with the children there. *Children will need close adult supervision. Caution kids to never share personal information, including last names.*
- Ask the chaplain or staff at the shelter or correctional facility for other ways your kids can minister on Mother's Day.
- Make Mother's Day cards for an elderly neighbor, someone who is homebound, or for women at a nursing home, veteran's home, or assisted living facility.

Testimonial

We arranged with the city to pick up trash around the downtown area and hosted a food drive for needy families in our community. The kids had a great time and want to do this sort of thing again. We treated them to a pizza lunch as a thank-you for giving. —Newman, California

_____ **Summer**

Make a Father's Day

Instructions

Father's Day can be a painful day for a father living in a shelter or correctional facility. Kids can add a spark of joy and love to his day by creating Father's Day cards just for him. Kids can use the card ideas from pages 20 - 25. When the cards are finished, they can use fine-tipped markers to print the words *Happy Father's Day from someone who cares for you—me* on the inside of the cards. They can even add a Scripture from Caring Cards (on pages 117 and 118). When the cards are finished, an adult can deliver them to the correctional facility or shelter.

Note

Call the chaplain at your local jail to ensure that sending cards is permitted. For security reasons your ministry opportunities may be very restricted. If cards are not allowed, ask the chaplain to suggest other ways your kids can minister to inmates on Father's Day.

Variation

Make Father's Day cards for an elderly neighbor, someone who is homebound, or for men at a nursing home, veteran's home, or assisted living facility.

Top It Off!

The last day of school is an exciting day for any child! Kids can help host a party that will be the icing on the cake (or the topping on the ice cream) to top off this special day.

Instructions
- Decide whom you will invite. Will it be a neighborhood party? A class party? A homeschool group party?
- Choose whether to serve cupcakes or ice cream.
- Kids and adults can work together to make invitations.
- Cut cardstock in half. On one side, print the kind of party (*It's an Ice Cream Party*, *It's a Cupcake Party*), the time, the location, and a phone number or email address for guests to RSVP. Ask guests to bring their favorite cupcake (or ice cream) topping.
- Decorate the invitation by drawing pictures of cupcakes or ice cream. Add stickers and other embellishments.

Variations
If your child can use the computer, help the child use a publishing program to make the invitations. Decorate the invitation by importing pictures, clip art, KidPix creations, or another art program.

Plan games or other activities for guests to do at the party. You can find game ideas at www.familyfun.com. Let your child choose his or her favorites.

Plan party favors such as tubes of sample-sized sunscreen, sponge balls (see Soaked in God's Love on p. 99), a bottle of liquid bubbles, or candy.

Purchase supplies
- For a cupcake party, purchase cake mix, oil, eggs, frosting, and cupcake liners.
- For an ice cream party, purchase a variety of ice cream flavors.
- Purchase balloons or other decorations.
- Have napkins, disposable plates or bowls, cups, utensils, and any items you need for the party favors.

Get ready
- Kids and adults should work together to make cupcakes (be sure to leave them unfrosted). Set out supplies and decorations, and wrap or bag the party favors. Be sure to include a Caring Card (see pp. 117-118) or other note expressing God's love in each bag.
- Kids and adults should pray before the party. Pray for each guest by name. Ask God to help each one sense and know His love.

Have Fun!
- Don't make a perfect party your goal. Make expressing God's love your topping on the cake (or ice cream)!

Testimonial
We threw a birthday party for children in a local homeless shelter. Twenty-three children were expected, however only about 15 were able to attend due to a flu outbreak. Each of the children,

along with some parents, were served sandwiches, chips, and cupcakes, and each child received a birthday present and candy bag. The children from our church decorated the cupcakes, wrapped the presents, and prepared the candy bags and sandwiches themselves. The party was a big hit and the kids from our church and the shelter want to get together again. For some of our kids, it was a real eye-opener to the realities of homelessness, and for some it was a thrilling opportunity to serve others. —Valdosta, Georgia

"A CHEERFUL LOOK BRINGS JOY TO THE HEART." PROVERBS 15:30

Soaked in God's Love

For a quick and clever welcome-to-summer gift, kids can make these simple and easy sponge balls. When loaded with water, they are a great way for friends to get wet and get soaked in God's love.

You'll Need
basic kitchen sponges
scissors
twist ties

Instructions
Cut the sponge in half. Stack the halves and twist them in the middle. Tightly wrap a twist tie around the middle. Be sure to twist it very tightly. Tie a string to a Caring Card (see pp. 117-118). On the back of the card print the words *May you be soaked in God's love this summer!* Attach the card to the sponge ball, and give it to your friend with a smile.

Hint
For a splash of color, use two different colors of sponges for each ball. Nylon sponges stay soft use after use, but they can also tear more easily.

Fall

Treat or Trick

Kids can go reverse trick or treating. Instead of gathering treats, they can go door to door to give out special treats to their neighbors.

You'll Need
small bags that will hold a candy bar and a message
candy bars
markers
scissors

Instructions Kids can decorate the bags using markers. Place a candy bar or another kind of candy into each bag. Tuck a verse card into each bag. (See Caring Cards on pages 117 and 118)

 CAUTION: Children will need close adult supervision for this activity. Kids should not be permitted to walk around the neighborhood alone, even if they know all the neighbors.

Holiday Place Mats

Placemats brighten any Thanksgiving table. Kids can make these colorful Thanksgiving placemats for elderly neighbors, people who are sick, residents of a nursing home or veterans' home, or people at a local soup kitchen.

You'll Need 12-by-18 inch pieces of construction paper
colorful paper
scissors
glue sticks
clear adhesive-backed plastic
glitter, confetti, paper punches, and other flat decorative items

Instructions
- Decorate the construction paper using an idea from Crepe Paper Cards, (p. 23) or Leaf Print Cards (p. 24). Use colors that are appropriate for the holiday.
- When your prints dry, cut out holiday shapes. Cut leaves for Thanksgiving; evergreen trees, snowmen, or ornament shapes for Christmas; and flower and cross shapes for Easter.
- Glue your shapes onto large pieces of construction paper.
- Print a note of encouragement or Scripture verse on the placemat. See Caring Cards (on pages 117 and 118) for ideas.
- Sprinkle some glitter, confetti, or paper punches over the top.
- Cut a 14-by-20-inch piece of adhesive-backed plastic, peel off the backing, and carefully lay it over the construction paper. Press and rub from the center outward to remove any bubbles. If you like, cover the back of the placemat with the adhesive plastic, too.
- Trim the edges with scissors.
- When you finish your placemat, pray that the person who uses it will sense and know God's love and care.

 CAUTION: An adult should supervise the delivery of the place mats. Personal contact between recipients and children should be kept to a minimum. Caution children never to share personal information, including their last names.

Variation Make placemats for Christmas, Easter, Valentine's Day, Mother's Day, Father's Day, or any other holiday or special occasion.

Season's Greetings

Think about people who are often forgotten at Christmas—people in an AIDS facility, patients in a veterans' hospital, and people in prison. What can be a better time to minister to lonely people than at Christmas, and what better message can be brought than the news of the Savior's birth!

You'll Need

new Christmas stockings
items to fill stockings
Christmas cards
Pen

Instructions

Decide where you would like to donate your Christmas stockings. Fill the stockings with small useful items such as pens, notepads; shaving gel, socks, packets of hot chocolate mix, candy, and gum. Kids can even make and add candy cane mice (see Not a Creature Was Stirring on p. 105). Let kids write notes on Christmas cards to the intended recipients. Place a card in each stocking.

Variations

- Go Christmas caroling as you deliver the stockings. If possible, visit with the recipients.
- Older children can fill stockings for young women at a home for unwed mothers. Consider donating a Christmas tree and decorating it with ornaments the kids have made.

 CAUTION: Be sure kids do not give any personal information (including last names) in their notes.

Happy Birthday Jesus!

Kids can organize and host a party to celebrate Jesus's birth. The party will minister to friends who don't know about Jesus, and it will give parents some time to do last minute Christmas shopping.

You'll Need

refreshments, such as a birthday cake, ice cream, punch, and candy
tubes of colored icing
birthday candles
party invitations

You'll Need (cont.)   pen
stamps
small wrapped gift for each child
birthday plates and napkins
confetti
plastic tablecloth
party hats and favors (optional)
roll of brown craft paper
craft paint
paintbrushes
foam stamps in Christmas shapes
paper towels
Bible
nativity set

Before the party:

- Kids can make a list of friends from the community they will invite to the party. Include children who don't know about Jesus.
- Prepare the menu. Plan to serve a plain birthday cake that kids can decorate with tubes of colored icing and birthday candles.
- Plan games and other activities to do at the party. Consider playing "Name That Christmas Tune," where one child hums a Christmas song for the others to guess. Older kids can make a Christmas Word Search for their guests to complete. Or print the words *Happy Birthday Jesus* on a poster. Provide paper and pencils, and lead your guests to see how many words they can make using the letters in the phrase.
- Gather supplies to make Christmas wrapping paper.

At the party:

- Welcome guests and give each a party hat and horn.
- Read the story of Jesus's birth and let the guests reenact it with a nativity set.
- Use tubes of icing and candles to decorate the birthday cake for Jesus.
- Sing "Happy Birthday" to Jesus before eating the cake. Serve other refreshments with the cake.
- Make Christmas wrapping paper. To make the wrapping paper, brush paint onto a foam stamp and stamp a design on brown paper. Provide damp paper towels for clean up.
- Play the games you prepared.
- When the party is over, thank each guest for coming.
- Invite kids to visit your church during the Christmas season.

Gift in a Jar

Kids can put together these easy-to-fix yummy snack mixes and give them to people they know. A special needs child would love to receive the Teddy Bear Snack Mix. An elderly neighbor would appreciate the Apple Walnut Oatmeal Mix. Any of these tasty mixes will make a wonderful gift when put in a fabric-covered jar or decorated plastic container, complete with a Scripture verse tag.

You'll Need

clean quart-sized glass jars with lids, such as those used in canning, or quart-sized plastic containers
colorful fabric
scissors
ribbon
card
hole punch
ingredients for the mix you will be making (See Jar Mixes on p. 119.)

Instructions

- Gather the ingredients for the recipe you select.
- Place the ingredients in a large bowl as directed and mix well.
- Place the mix into the prepared jar.
- Make a card for your jar, giving the directions for using the mix. Include a personal message or Scripture verse on the other side of the card. Punch a hole in one corner of the card, and thread a length of ribbon through the hole.
- Decorate the jar by creating a fabric lid. Trace around the jar lid to make a circle on the fabric. The circle should be about twice as large as the lid. Cut it out.
- Place the lid on the jar and the fabric circle on top of the lid. Secure the fabric by tying the ribbon with the card to neck of the jar, just under the lid.

Variation

Make several gift jars. Give them to neighbors, veterans' home residents, or homebound neighbors. Use fabric with a Christmas pattern to decorate the lids. Make a Christmas card to go with each jar.

Hint

If you are filling a used jar, be sure that it is clean and sanitized. Use a dishwasher or boil the jar and lid in a large pot of water for at least 5 minutes.

 CAUTION: Be sure the recipient of your Gift in a Jar doesn't have any diet restrictions.

The Light of Christmas

Kids can make colorful craft foam Christmas lights to remind people that Jesus is the light of the world!

You'll Need craft foam in a variety of bright colors
scissors
black ¾-inch binder clips
Black cording

Instructions
- Photocopy the light bulb pattern (p. 133) and cut it out. Trace the pattern onto the craft foam. Cut out the foam bulb. Attach a binder clip to the base of the bulb. Remove the handles by pinching the sides together and sliding the feet out of the grooves. Thread a 12-inch length of black cording through the clip. Tie a double knot around the clip. Thread on a Caring Card (pp. 117-118), and then tie another double knot at the ends to make a loop for hanging.
- On the back of the card, print the words *Jesus is the Light of the world.*
- Allow children to deliver their foam lights to neighbors, teachers, friends, people who are homebound, children at a hospital, clerks at a store, or anyone in need.

Testimonial *Our kids decided to make birthday bags to benefit the local food bank. The children had a fun time decorating the bags and making cards. We put the finished bags on the altar and dedicated them during the Sunday morning service before delivering the bags to the food bank. They were so happy to see us. We filled up the entire office! It's exciting to see God working through our children.*
—Litchfield, Connecticut

Caroling

Kids can make these colorful carolers and give them as gifts when they go Christmas caroling. Each caroler can serve as a reminder of the visit and of God's tender care.

You'll Need toilet paper tube
cardstock or scrapbook paper in bright patterns or colors
cardstock or scrapbook paper in light, medium, and dark skin tones
felt (optional)
fine-tipped black marker
red or pink pencil
glue stick
an old, colorful child's sock
yarn or ribbon

Instructions
- For each caroler, cut the colorful paper into a 4 ½–by-6-inch rectangle. Wrap the paper around a toilet paper tube, and glue it in place.
- Cut a 1½-inch circle from the skin-toned paper. Use the marker to add eyes and a mouth. (To make a singing mouth, draw an O shape.) If you like, add rosy cheeks with the pink or red pencil.
- Cut a 1½-by-2-inch rectangle from the colorful paper, and fold it in half to be the caroler's songbook.
- Cut out two 1-inch paper or felt mittens. Glue the tips of the mittens to the outside and bottom of the songbook, then glue the mittens to the caroler.

- To make a hat for the caroler, cut the sock at the ankle. Throw away the foot portion. Fold one end of the sock tube into a cuff and stretch the sock over the caroler's head. Tie the top of the hat with yarn or ribbon.
- Attach a Caring Card to the caroler.

You can also use construction paper to make the carolers, but cardstock and scrapbook paper will resist fading.

Hint

Not a Creature Was Stirring

Kids can make cute Christmas mice that carry the message of the Christmas season and a sweet treat, too!

You'll Need

felt in two different colors
one miniature pom-pom
googly eyes
glue
candy

Instructions

- Photocopy mouse patterns on page 133. Use the patterns to cut a body and ears from felt.
- Cut two parallel slits near the center of the body piece. The slits should be about 1-inch long and ½-inch apart. Use the lines on the body pattern as a guide.
- Thread the bowtie-shaped piece of felt through the slits. This will represent the ears.
- Glue on a pom-pom nose and googly eyes.
- Slide a ribbon under the mouse and tuck it through the ear loop beneath the body. Use the ribbon to attach the mouse to a bag, bar, or stick of wrapped candy of your choice.
- Photocopy a John 3:16 Caring Card (see pp. 117-118). Print the words *Jesus Is the Reason for the Season* on the back of the card. Hole punch to thread with the ribbon and tie to attach to mouse and candy.

Christmas Cheer

At Christmas kids can share the love of Christ by participating in a toy drive. Angel Tree, Operation Christmas Child, and the Salvation Army collect toys for children in need.

Angel Tree—Sponsored by Prison Fellowship, Angel Tree is a ministry that reaches out to the children and families of inmates with the love of Christ. Through the Angel Tree program, volunteers purchase and deliver gifts to the children of inmates in their parents' names. Children can collect presents for Angel Tree children, and make cards or special gifts to send with the presents. For more information about the Angel Tree program, visit www.angeltree.org.

Operation Christmas Child—A project of Samaritan's Purse, Operation Christmas Child provide joy, hope, and opportunities for local believers to tell the children about Jesus Christ. Each year, Samaritan's Purse donates millions of shoeboxes filled with toys and other gifts to children around the world. Kids can collect items and pack them into shoeboxes. They can include personal notes and photos of themselves or their families. Kids can also pray that the children who receive the shoeboxes will come to know Jesus Christ as their Lord and Savior. For more information about Operation Christmas Child, how to pack shoeboxes, and where to drop them off, visit www.samaritanspurse.org/OCC

Salvation Army—Providing for needy children at Christmas is one of the many projects of the Salvation Army. Contact your local Salvation Army to see how kids can participate. For information, go to www.salvationarmy.org.

Variation   Many organizations sponsor toy drives for the children of those serving in the military. Contact the military base in your region for information.

Testimonial   *Our group of 15 kids collected 172 pounds of food to be distributed through the church food pantry.*
— Kennewick, Washington

"THANKS BE TO GOD FOR HIS INDESCRIBABLE GIFT." (2 CORINTHIANS 9:15, NIV)

Hearts a Blooming

Everyone loves to receive flowers, especially ones that never die. Kids can make and give these colorful paper flowers to show God's love at Valentines' Day.

You'll Need   white, pink, and/or red cardstock
red, pink, or white Chenille Craft stems
scissors
gel glue or tacky glue
ribbon
Optional: heart stickers, heart paper punches, glue

Instructions   • Cut the cardstock into heart shapes. Use the template on page 130 as a guide.
• Choose two hearts. On one heart, cut a slit from the *V* at the top halfway to the bottom tip of the heart. On the other heart, cut a slit from the bottom tip halfway to the *V*.
• Take the second heart and hold it above the first heart. Line up the slits, and slide the two hearts together.
• Glue a chenille stem to the bottom tip of your heart flower.

- If you like, add heart stickers or heart-shaped paper punches to the flowers. You can also cut paper into leaf shapes and glue them to your stems.
- When you have several hearts, arrange them in a vase. Use tissue paper or paper shreds to help hold the stems in place.
- Wrap ribbon around the vase, tie it into a bow, and add a Caring Card (see pp. 117-118). Deliver your vase of flowers with a smile.

Hint

Cut heart shapes with a die cutter if you have access to one.

Variations

Kids can try the following Variations to add some color to their papers before they make the bouquets:

Make marbleized hearts using the technique described in Marbleized Cards (see p. 20). Use red food coloring and white or pink cardstock.

Make spin art hearts using the technique described in Spin Art Cards (see p. 24). Use red, pink, or white tempera paint. When the paint dries, make the bouquets as described above.

Out of This World!

Kids can give these clever candy rockets on Valentine's Day to let people know God's love is "out of this world!"

You'll Need

construction paper
scissors
clear tape
roll of Life Savers or other round candy
Chocolate kiss candy
red tissue paper or crepe paper
tacky glue

Instructions

- Cut a piece of construction paper to fit around your roll of candy. Print the words *God's love is out of this world!* on the paper, and tape it to the roll.
- Glue a chocolate candy kiss to one end of the roll. Glue a thin strip of red tissue paper to the other end.
- When the glue dries, fringe the end of the tissue paper to make it look like flames.
- Attach a Caring Card (see pp. 117-118) to the body of the rocket and give it to a friend. The John 3:16 Caring Card is a good choice.

Variation

Wrap the candy with red, white, and blue paper for a Fourth of July theme, or red and white paper for a Canada day theme.

God's Heart Beats for You

In this Valentine's gift, the hand is quicker than the eye.

You'll Need
cardstock
scissors
decorative Valentine's Day pencil or a dowel stick
tape
markers

Instructions
- Cut a 4-inch heart from cardstock. Use the heart pattern on page 130 as a guide.
- On one side of the heart, draw a large heart in the center. On the other side, draw a small heart in the center. Color the hearts.
- Tape a pencil or dowel to the bottom tip of the paper heart. Be careful not to cover your drawings.
- Hold the stick between the palms of your hands and rub your hands back and forth to make the stick roll backwards and forwards. You should see a beating heart.
- Finally, use curling ribbon to attach a Caring Card to the stick. On the back of the card, print the words *God's heart beats for you!*
- When you give your "beating heart" on Valentine's Day, show the recipient how it works.

Hint
Purchase packages of 12-inch dowels at craft stores or major retail stores

Variations
Add a decorative border to your heart card: Cut two 4-inch hearts from white cardstock and one 5-inch heart from pink or red cardstock. Glue the white hearts to both sides of the pink or red heart. If you like, trim the large heart with pinking or decorative edge scissors.

Deliver your Beating Heart with a Valentine cookie or candy.

Chapter 4

Kids Can Minister Anytime

Check this list for a number of quick and easy projects kids can do anytime.

Kids can

- Smile. It may be the only smile some people see all week. "A cheerful look brings joy to the heart" (Proverbs 15:30*a*)

- Say quick, silent prayers for the people they see during the day.

- Let others go in front of them in line.

- Open or hold a door open for others.

- Get a shopping cart for the people who come into a store behind them.

- Return a shopping cart for others.

- Include a Caring Card when they trade stuffed animals or toys with friends.

- Give Christian CDs and/or DVDs to friends.

- Loan paper or pencils to kids at school.

- Invite people to church.

- Do lawn work such as rake leaves for free.

- Take the neighbors' newspapers to their porches.

- Start an after-school homework help group for younger kids in the neighborhood.

- Hold umbrellas for others.

- Practice the "Ministry of Manners." They can say please, thank you, excuse me, and other polite words. ("be kind and gentle toward all people" Titus 3:2*b*.)

- Ask parents to help send encouraging e-cards through constanthope.org.

- Pray that the makers of the children's TV shows, movies, video, and Internet games will come to know Jesus as their Savior and that they will use their talents God has given them for His glory.

- Send cards or e-cards to servicemen or servicewomen, homeless shelters, family shelters, nursing homes, missionaries, inmates, and to others who might not receive cards or letters.

- Offer to put flowers on the graves of the loved ones of people who are homebound or in a nursing home.

- Clean up a cemetery. Many cemeteries do not have money to hire people to weed, mow, and clean.

- Organize a Saturday workday at a local park.

- Volunteer to sort clothes and food at a local food pantry or clothes closet.

- Volunteer to serve a meal at a local homeless shelter. *Caution: Adult supervision is required for this activity.*

- Go caroling at a nursing home. It doesn't just have to be at Christmas.

- Pick up the trash in the community.

- Clean up any graffiti in the area.

- With permission, plant flowers at a community park.

- Teach a younger child how to play a sport.

- Hold a garage sale and give the money to missions or non-profit organizations.

- Recycle devotional magazines by putting them in doctors' offices, bus and train stations, truck stops, etc. (Ask your church for outdated materials.)

- Start a diaper drive for a local crisis pregnancy center .

- Use sidewalk chalk to create maze-like trails around the neighborhood. Have the trails lead to driveways where there is a special message about Jesus. If neighbors live in an apartment, children can make posters that tell about Jesus and hang them on apartment doors. If kids don't live in a neighborhood, they can make a sign to display in their yards.

- Distribute small tracts or verse cards (see Caring Cards on pages 117 and 118) to friends in the neighborhood, store clerks, and other people in the community. *Caution: Adult supervision is strongly recommended for this activity. Children should not be permitted to speak with strangers alone.*

- Donate gently used toys to needy children or children who have been displaced from their homes because of a fire or other natural disaster. Make sure the toys are clean, in good condition, and have all necessary parts.

- Be friends. Kids can pray and ask God to show them people who need friends. When God gives His answer, they can pray for the people and spend time with them. They can invite them to their homes, send them cards and notes in the mail, send emails, go to the movies together, or invite them to church.

Testimonial *Our children provided eighteen Happy Birthday Bash Bags to be distributed to low-income families in our community.*
— Russellville, Kentucky

Chapter 5

Kids Can Minister Anywhere

Are you interested in taking kids on a mini missions trip, but not sure where to start? First, look around the community. Is there a nursing home? A fire hall? A police station? A family or women's shelter? A hospital or clinic? A park? Ask God to show you and your kids a site or a group of people who could benefit from a touch of His love. You will want to remember that a mini missions trip does not necessarily require a craft, though there are many suggestions here. Encourage kids to share Christ's love, and let them know that assisting ministry leaders is enough. When gives you an idea, you also can look through the ministry projects in this book to find ways you and your kids might help. You can also find some suggestions below.

Next, contact the site and introduce yourself. If you plan to take a group of kids, tell what group you represent. Share your ministry ideas, and ask if they are appropriate. Accept suggestions, and ask if your family or group can minister in other ways. Before making a commitment to help, visit the site to make sure it is safe and appropriate for children.

When you have chosen your site and your ministry, refer to the Mini Missions Trip Checklist to help you plan. Also be sure to refer to the Safety Checklists on page 115.

Mini missions trip to a nursing home or veteran's home

- Children can collect items for Comfort Kits (p. 37) and assemble the kits. They can also gather supplies for Celebrate the Seasons (p. 32). At the site, kids can deliver the Comfort Kits and decorate bulletin boards according to the suggestions in Celebrate the Seasons.
- Kids can give a recital. Refer to Encore! (p. 38) for tips and ideas.
- Children can make birdfeeders and birdbaths for the facility. See Bird Watching (p. 39). They can also gather supplies for making bird-watching scrapbooks. At the site, children can hang the feeders and set up the birdbaths. They can also work one-on-one with seniors to make bird-watching scrapbooks for the seniors to keep.

Mini missions trip to a hospital or clinic

- Kids can prepare or collect items from The Waiting Game, Worth the Wait, God Bless You, Laughter Is the Best Medicine, Slipper Socks, Tooth Pillow, or other projects from pages 44-48. At the site, the kids can deliver the items they made or collected. They can also pray with families. If possible, arrange a tour for the kids.

Mini missions trip to a food bank

- Kids can sponsor a food drive for a local food bank. See Stocking Up on page 51. They can also follow the suggestions in Paper or Plastic? (p. 50) to decorate bags for the pantry's ministry. Along with the bags, they can make gifts for children of food pantry clients. See the Variations under Paper or Plastic? If possible, kids can stock shelves or fill bags with food when they deliver the food and other items. They might also be able to take part in a tour.

Testimonial

Our group, after gathering food items for 3 weeks, packed bags for 20 people in our community, who receive prepared meals during the week but struggle to have enough on the weekends. We started out with our eyes set on packing a gallon sealable plastic bag for them but, as it ended up, we packed each one a whole grocery bag full of food. The girls also prepared cards for each bag. We had a great time and were most blessed. We love missions! —Gaffney, South Carolina

Mini missions trip to a family shelter

- Children can collect items for Care Kits (p. 52), prepare games for the children at the shelter (Let the Games Begin on p. 74), and make cards for the families (see pp. 20-25). At the shelter, they can deliver the cards and Care Kits. They can also play games with the children.
- Older kids can sponsor a drive to collect books for the shelter (see Read to Me on p. 76). Kids can deliver the books, and read to the children.

Mini missions trip to a childcare facility

Children can sponsor a drive to collect books or other needed items for a child care center (see Read to Me on p. 76). They can make several batches of Easy Dough for the facility also (p. 76). While at the site, older children can read to the preschoolers. Younger children can work with adults to plant flowers or do any other beautification project. The group can also clean the center's vehicle (see Scrub-a-Dub on p. 79). If permissible, they can serve a snack to the kids. And, while the preschoolers enjoy their snacks, the kids can perform a puppet show (see Show and Tell on p. 70).

Mini missions trip to a fire hall or police station

Kids can take a trip to a fire hall or police station. Before the trip, they can bake cookies (see Cookies, Cookies! on p. 70). Kids might also make key chains to give to the fire fighters or police officers (see Keychain Kindness on p. 73). At the site, kids can deliver the cookies and key chains. If permissible, they might also Scrub-a-Dub a vehicle (p. 79), or take part in a tour.

Mini missions trip to a community event

With permission from the event organizers, kids can distribute water bottles (see Cool Message on p. 79); sunscreen, lip balm and hand sanitizer (see That's Just What I Needed! on p. 82); and offer free Bibles or tracts. Before the event, kids can sponsor a drive to collect the needed items. At the site, kids can carry baskets or pull wagons containing the items and offer them to staff and visitors. Kids can also learn to create Balloon Animals (p. 78) and make them for visitors.

CAUTION: Close adult supervision is required for this trip. Each adult should supervise no more than two children. The children should stay with the adult at all times.

NOTE: The previous ideas are suggestions only. Work with the appropriate individual at your ministry site to determine the best ways your family or group can help.

Mini Missions Trip Checklist

❑ Pray, asking God for guidance.

❑ Survey different agencies or locations where your group can serve. Visit potential sites. Before making a final selection, be sure the destination is safe and appropriate for children. If you have children or chaperones with special needs, make sure the site is accessible as well.

❑ Check your church or school calendar for available dates. Confirm a date with your chosen ministry site.

❑ Estimate the number of children who will participate and enlist an appropriate number of adult chaperones. *You should have a minimum of two adult chaperones and a ratio of at least one adult for every eight children.*

❑ Enlist an adult to take pictures during the trip.

❑ Make appropriate travel arrangements and pay any necessary deposits.

❑ Make sure your group or organization has proper insurance coverage.

❑ Plan your budget, including an approximate cost for each individual involved. Remember to include supply expenses, travel expenses, publicity expenses, en route expenses (meals or other), and any on site expenses. Determine how much your church, school, or organization will provide and how much each child and adult chaperone will pay. If necessary, recruit sponsors or plan fundraisers to help offset costs.

❑ If you will promote the trip through newsletters, fliers, or web sites, meet with the appropriate individuals to establish and implement a publicity plan.

❑ If you will collect items to take to the ministry site, make plans to publicize the drive and collect the items.

❑ If you will make items to distribute, prepare for those.

❑ If you will perform at the site, choose your material and schedule rehearsal dates, times, and locations.

Six Weeks Before the Trip

❑ Prepare a letter to parents that will describe the trip and give details such as the date, time, place, cost (if any), and any other important information. Prepare a permission slip for parents to sign before their children go on any trip.

One Month Before the Trip

❑ Promote the trip. Begin to train and prepare your group for the event. Always include prayer in your training and preparation!

❑ Distribute information letters to parents and guardians.

❑ Promote the event in your church, school, or organization's newsletter, bulletin, and web site.

❑ If you are collecting items, make and distribute posters or fliers. Prepare and set out collection boxes.

❑ Obtain the permission form approved by your organization. A sample form is on page 116. If your chosen ministry site has its own required permission form, obtain copies of this form as well.

❑ Request checks for remaining transportation costs or other known expenses from your group's financial officer.

Two Weeks Before the Trip

- ❏ Train and prepare your kids for the event. Continue to pray.
- ❏ Confirm who will be chaperones.
- ❏ Distribute permission forms to parents and guardians.
- ❏ Confirm your trip with the contact person at your ministry site. Ask if there is any new information or changes that might affect your trip.
- ❏ Confirm your travel arrangements.

One Week Before the Trip

- ❏ Meet with the adult chaperones to discuss logistics for the trip. Spend time praying for the event.
- ❏ Prepare nametags for both kids and chaperones. Nametags should include **only first names.**
- ❏ Collect signed permission forms and fees, if any, from parents and guardians.
- ❏ Determine the amount of petty cash you will need for miscellaneous expenses and emergencies. Make arrangements to collect the cash from your church, school, or organization's financial officer.
- ❏ If you don't already have a well-stocked first aid kit, purchase or prepare one.

Day Before the Event

- ❏ Schedule to pick up the transportation vehicle(s), if necessary.

Event Day

- ❏ Arrive at the chosen meeting site early.
- ❏ Pray with your group and the adult chaperones.
- ❏ Be sure to take:
  - a first aid kit
  - a fully charged cell phone and cell phone charger
  - the kids' medical consent forms
  - the emergency contact information for each child
  - any medication or equipment for children with special medical needs
  - a list of participants
  - petty and emergency cash
  - nametags for adults and kids
- ❏ If you collected or made items for the trip, gather the items and take them too.
- ❏ Call your contact person at the ministry site and notify that person of your estimated arrival time.
- ❏ If you recruited an adult to take pictures, obtain approval from your contact person before taking pictures on site.
- ❏ Have fun!

One Week After the Trip

- ❏ Send thank-you notes to your contact person, the ministry site, and the people within your church or organization who helped make the trip possible. Prepare cards for the group to sign or let each child make his own. See the card suggestions on pages 20-25.
- ❏ Meet with your group to talk about the trip. Share the pictures, encourage the kids to talk about how the trip affected them, and pray for the ministry site.

Mini Missions Trip Safety Checklist

❑ **Research your destination.** Before selecting a missions trip site, be sure the destination is safe and appropriate for children. Call ahead and visit the site in advance. View the site from a safety perspective. If you have children or sponsors with special needs, make sure the site is accessible as well.

❑ **Obtain a signed permission form for each participating child.** The permission form should include: the date of the trip, the destination and its address, the departure and return times, a list of attending adults, and an emergency contact number for each child. The permission form should also include consent for medical care, emergency contact numbers for the parent or guardian, and a list of medications that the child may need to take while on the trip. You can find a sample permission form on page 116.

❑ **Maintain safe adult to child ratios.** You should have a minimum of two adult chaperones and a ratio of at **least** one adult for every eight children.

❑ **Take health and safety supplies with you.** Carry a cell phone and its charger, a well-stocked first aid kit, medical consent forms, and emergency contact information for each child. Also take any medication or equipment for children with special medical needs such as asthma, diabetes, or other conditions.

❑ **Take a list of participants.** Use the list to conduct frequent head counts.

❑ **Provide identification tags for each chaperone.** These should be bright and colorful so they are easily recognized. Consider making matching shirts for chaperones or having chaperones wear the same color clothing each day of the trip.

SAFETY CHECKLIST FOR KIDS

❑ Identify the kids in your group with special stickers or matching shirts. If the children wear nametags, print first names only.

❑ Establish a buddy system. Tell kids to stay with their buddies throughout the trip. Children with special needs may need an adult buddy.

❑ Make sure kids are familiar with the adult chaperones. Arrange a time before the trip for children to meet the chaperones.

❑ Make sure there is a booster seat or seat belt for each child.

❑ When you arrive at the site, identify a place for children to go if they become separated from the group.

❑ Teach the kids what to do if they become separated from the group:
  • Stay in the place where they last saw the group or go to the designated "lost" area.
  • Tell them **never** to leave the area with a person they do not know.

❑ Reassure kids that if they do become lost, you will be looking for them and that you will not leave without them.

The above information is general in nature and should not be substituted for professional advice.

Permission Form

Our group, _____ , is planning a trip to _____

Date _____ Time _____

Location _____

Telephone Number _____

Arrangements for transportation:

Time and place of departure _____

Time and place of return _____

Mode of transportation _____

Leaders accompanying the children:

Name(s) _____

Each child will need:

Equipment and clothing _____

Expenses _____

In case of an emergency, the leader will notify:

Name _____ Telephone Number _____

who will immediately notify a parent or guardian.

Leader's signature _____ Telephone Number _____

- -

Parent/Guardian Permission Form

Please return this portion to the group leader by _____

My child, _____

has permission to participate in: _____

During the activity, I (we) can be reached at:

Address _____

Telephone Number 1 _____ Telephone Number 2 _____

If I (we) cannot be reached in the event of an emergency, the following person is authorized to act in my (our) behalf:

Name _____ Relationship to participant _____

Address _____

Telephone Number 1 _____ Telephone Number 2 _____

Physician's Name _____ Telephone Number _____

Additional remarks: _____

Required medications my child may take while on the trip: _____

In the event of an emergency, I hereby give permission for first aid and emergency medical treatment to be secured for my child.

Parent or guardian's signature _____ Date _____

This permission form is a SAMPLE ONLY. Use the form approved by your organization.

Appendix-Caring Cards

Photocopy the cards onto cardstock and cut them out. Kids can include an appropriate card when they give their ministry gifts. You can find the Spanish versions of these cards on the following page.

May the Lord bless you and take good care of you. May the Lord smile on you and be gracious to you. May the Lord look on you with favor and give you his peace. (Numbers 6:24–26 NIV)

When I'm afraid, I will trust in you. (Psalm 56:3)

Give thanks to the Lord, because he is good. His faithful love continues forever. (Psalm 106:1)

The Lord is faithful and will keep of his promises … loving toward everything he has made. (Psalm 145:13)

Trust in the Lord with all your heart. Do not depend on your own understanding. In all your ways remember him. Then he will make your paths smooth and straight. Proverbs 3:5–6

He gives strength to those who are tired. He gives power to those who are weak. Isaiah 40:29

God loved the world so much that he gave his one and only Son. Anyone who believes in him will not die but will have eternal life. John 3:16

I thank my God every time I remember you. Philippians 1:3

From someone who cares—me!

I'm praying for you.

Turn all your worries over to him. He cares about you. 1 Peter 5:7

Made with love and prayer.

Caring Cards (cont'd)

Cuando siento miedo, pongo en ti mi confianza. (Salmo 56:3 NVI)

El Señor te bendiga y te guarde; el Señor te mire con agrado y te extienda su amor; el Señor te muestre su favor y te conceda la paz. (Números 6:24–26 NVI)

Fiel es el Señor en todas sus promesas y leal en todo lo que hace. (Salmo 145:3)

Den gracias al Señor, porque él es bueno; su gran amor perdura para siempre. (Salmo 106:1 NVI)

El da esfuerzo al cansado, y multiplica las fuerzas al que no tiene ningunas. Isaías 40:29, VRV, 1960

Confía de todo corazón en el Señor y no en tu propia inteligencia. Ten presente al Señor en todo lo que hagas, y él te llevará por el camino recto. Proverbios 3:5, 6, Dios Habla Hoy

Doy gracias a mi Dios cada vez que me acuerdo de ustedes. Filipenses 1:3, NIV

Porque tanto amó Dios al mundo, que dio a su Hijo unigénito, para que todo el que cree en él no se pierda, sino que tenga vida eterna. Juan 3:16 NVI

Estoy orando por usted (or ustedes).

De alguien que se interesa por ti –¡yo!

Hecho con amor y oración.

Depositen en él toda ansiedad, porque él cuida de ustedes. 1 Pedro 5:7

Hot Cocoa Mix

4 cups nonfat dry milk powder
1½ cups sugar
1 cup cocoa powder
1 cup powdered nondairy creamer
pinch of salt
1 bag mini marshmallows
½ cup chocolate chips (optional)
sandwich-sized zipper-topped plastic bags

In a large bowl, mix the first five ingredients. You may add chocolate chips if you wish. Fill clean quart-sized jars three quarters full with hot cocoa mix. For each jar of mix, place 1-cup mini marshmallows in a sandwich-sized plastic bag, or wrap them in plastic wrap. Place a bag inside each jar and replace jar lids. To each jar attach a card with directions for serving.

Apple Walnut Oatmeal Mix

1 package (7 ounces) dried apples, chopped
18 ounces quick cooking oats
3 ounces powdered non-dairy creamer
½ cup firmly packed brown sugar
½ cup chopped walnuts
pinch of salt
2 teaspoons cinnamon

Mix all the ingredients in a large bowl. Place into quart-sized jars. To each jar attach a card with directions for serving.

Hot Cocoa Mix

Directions: Blend ¼ cup cocoa mix with ¾ cup boiling water. Stir well. Add marshmallows.

Apple Walnut Oatmeal Mix

Directions: To make oatmeal stir ⅔ cup boiling water into ½ cup mix. Stir and let stand until thickened.

---

4 Bean Soup Mix

¼ cup each dried kidney beans, black beans, navy beans, and split peas
3 tablespoons dried minced onion
¼ cup pearl barley
2 teaspoons Italian seasoning
1 bay leaf
1 tablespoon beef bouillon granules

Mix beans in a large bowl and spoon into a quart-sized jar. In a small bowl mix the remaining ingredients and pour into a small zipper-topped plastic bag. Place the bag inside the jar. Attach the card with directions to the jar.

4 Bean Soup

Directions: In 3-quart container, soak beans in 7 cups of water overnight. In the morning bring the beans and water to a boil. Reduce heat and add seasoning packet. Cover and simmer 2 hours. Optional: Add a 16 ounce can of tomatoes and simmer an additional 30 minutes.

Teddy Bear Snack Mix

2 cups bear-shaped graham snacks, any flavor
2 cups mini chocolate sandwich cookies
4 cups caramel popcorn
1 cup candy-coated chocolate pieces
1 cup gummy bears

Mix all ingredients in a large bowl. Put into quart-sized jars.

Teddy Bear Snack Mix

Mix all ingredients in a large bowl. Put into quart-sized jars.

Peanut Butter Kiss Cookies

½ cup butter
½ cup sugar
½ cup brown sugar
½ cup peanut butter
¼ teaspoon salt

1 egg
1½ cups flour
½ teaspoon baking soda
1 teaspoon vanilla
1 small bag chocolate kisses, unwrapped

Cream butter, sugar, and brown sugar together. Add peanut butter, egg, and vanilla. Mix well. In another bowl mix flour, salt, and baking soda. Add to peanut butter mixture. Roll into 1-inch balls and place onto a greased cookie sheet. Bake at 350 degrees for 8 minutes. Take cookies out of the oven. Place a kiss in the center of each cookie. Return the cookies to the oven and continue baking for about two more minutes or until cookies are golden.

Carrot Cake in a Jar

2⅔ cups sugar
⅔ cup shortening
4 eggs
⅔ cup water
2 teaspoons vanilla
3½ cups flour

1 teaspoon baking powder
2 teaspoons baking soda
1 teaspoon salt
2 teaspoons cinnamon
2 cups peeled, grated carrots
⅔ cup chopped nuts

Preheat oven to 325 degrees. Grease six one-pint, wide-mouthed canning jars. In a large bowl, cream together sugar and shortening. Add eggs, water, and vanilla. Mix well. In a separate bowl mix the flour, baking powder, baking soda, salt, and cinnamon. Add the dry ingredients to the creamed ingredients. Mix well. Gently stir in carrots and nuts. Place 1 cup of batter in each of the prepared jars. Place the jars on a cookie sheet and place them in the oven. Bake 55 minutes. Removing one jar at a time, immediately place sterilized canning seals and rings on the jars. This will seal the jar. The sealed jar will keep the cake fresh up to a month.

Pumpkin Bread

1⅔ cups flour
1½ cups sugar
1 teaspoon baking soda
½ teaspoon salt
½ teaspoon baking powder
½ teaspoon cinnamon
¼ teaspoon nutmeg

¼ teaspoon ground cloves
1 cup cooked or canned pumpkin
½ cup vegetable oil
½ cup water
2 eggs
½ cup chopped nuts (optional)

Preheat oven to 350 degrees. Mix flour, sugar, baking soda, salt, baking powder, and spices together. Add pumpkin, oil, water, and eggs. Stir well. Fold in nuts if desired. Pour the batter into a greased and floured loaf pan. Bake 1 hour.

Jokes

What do sea monsters eat? (fish and ships)

What do you get when you cross a snowman and a wolf? (frostbite)

What building has the most stories? (a library)

Why do sharks swim only in salt water? (Pepper makes them sneeze.)

What is black and white and red all over? (a zebra wearing too much lipstick)

What goes ha ha ha ha plop? (someone laughing his head off)

What is large and gray and goes around in circles? (an elephant in a revolving door)

What did the grape say to the elephant? (Nothing; grapes can't talk.)

Why don't elephants ride bikes? (They don't have thumbs to ring the bell.)

What did the math book say to the history book? (I have problems.)

When is a car not a car? (when it turns into a driveway)

What starts with P, ends with E, and has thousands of letters in it? (post office)

What did the cherry tree say to the farmer? (Quit picking on me.)

What do you say when you meet a two-headed monster? (Hello, hello.)

What happens when you cross the road? (You meet a chicken.)

What do you do when an elephant sneezes? (Get out of the way.)

What was the worm doing in the cornfield? (Going in one ear and out the other.)

Tissue Cover Pattern

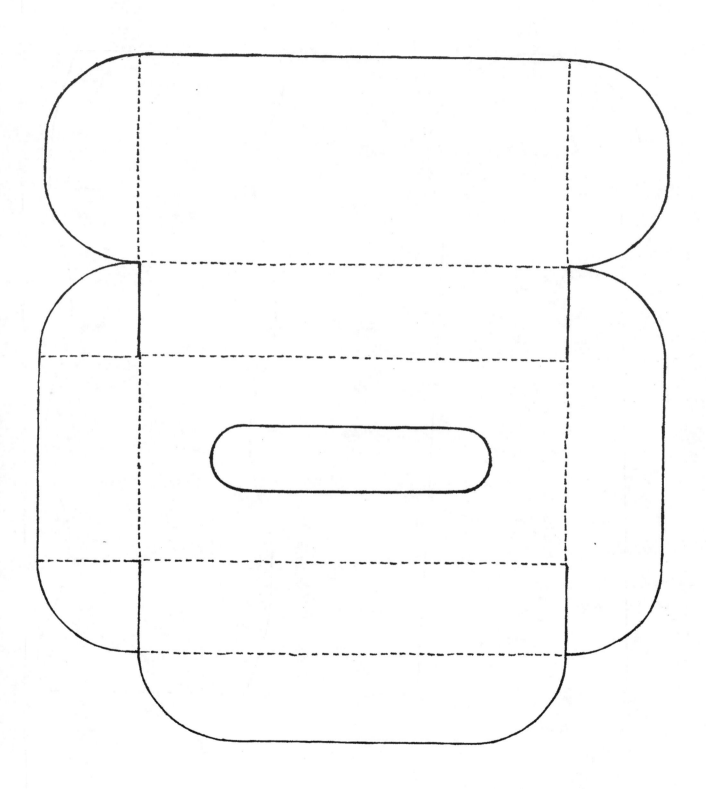

Bookmarks

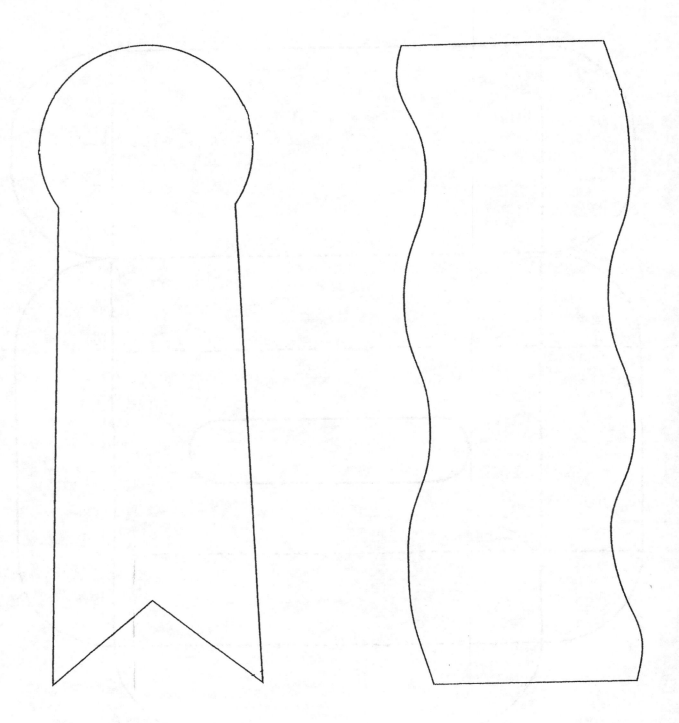

Animal Menagerie

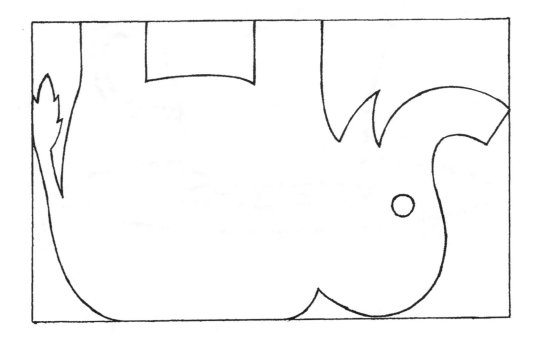

*Inside this kit
you will find:*

Bubbles—

to stay young

A cup—

for when yours is overflowing
or needs filling

A tea bag—

for when you need comfort

Two hugs—

one to keep and one to give

A heart—

because God loves you

Tooth Pillow and Pocket Patterns

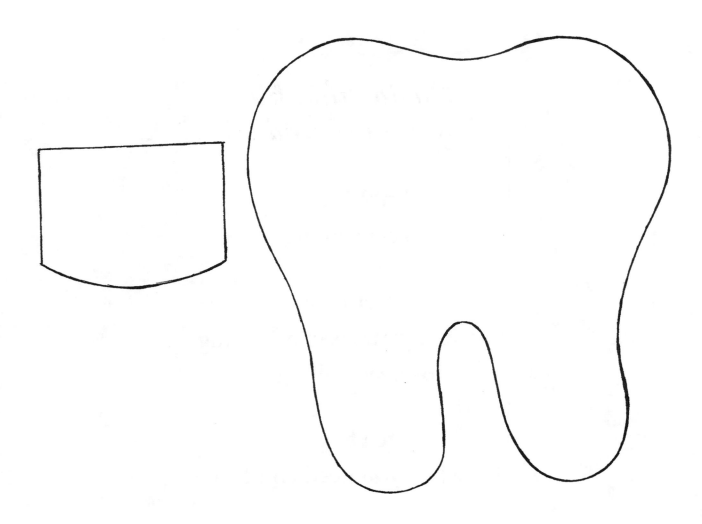

Inside this Survival Kit you will find:

A cup—
for when yours needs filling

A glue stick—
for when you need help holding things together

A tea bag—
for when you need comfort

Bubbles—
for when you need joy

A pencil sharpener—
for when you need to stay sharp

A hug—
for when you need one

A heart—
because God loves you

Thank you for being a great teacher!

Heart Pattern

Paper Glider

- Fold the paper in half vertically (the paper will be long and skinny). Unfold.
- Fold the bottom two corners of the paper towards the centerfold line so that the corners touch about 1 inch from the bottom edge of the paper.
- Fold up the bottom edge about ¾ of an inch. Repeat 7 times.
- Flip the paper over and fold the glider in half.
- Fold down the top wing about ¾-inch from the centerfold.
- Flip the glider over and repeat the previous step to make the second wing.
- Flip the glider so that the folds are facedown. Make wing tips by folding up the end of each wing at an angle. The wing tip should be about ½-inch tall in the back and should angle to a point at the front (the fold end) of the wing.

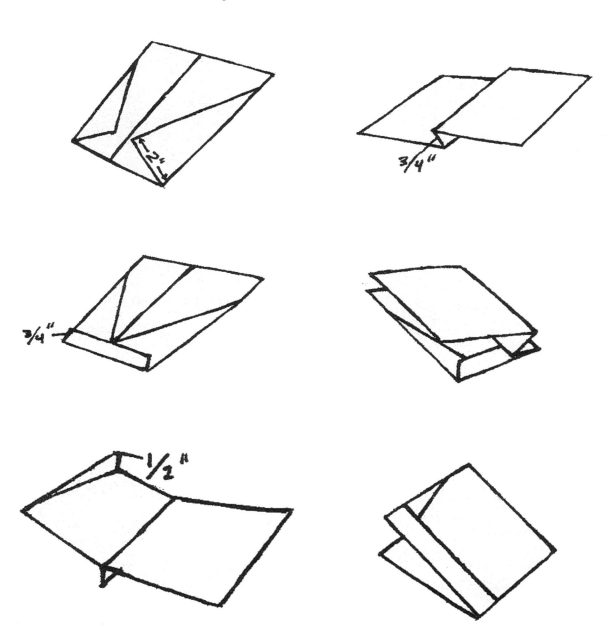

131

Lightbulb Pattern

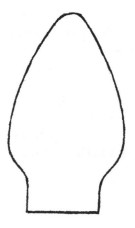

Pop-Up Card

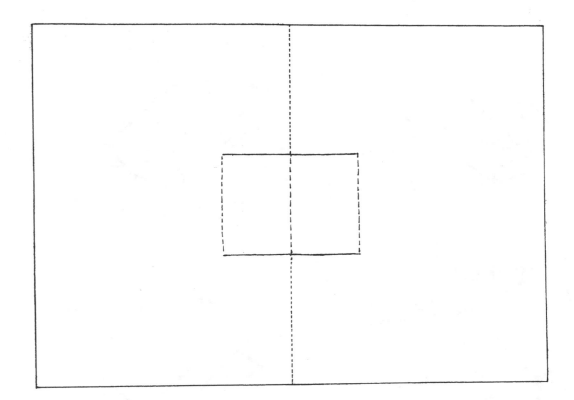

Mouse Patterns

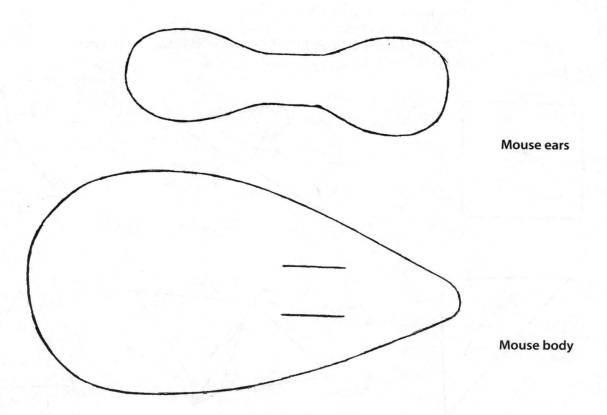

Mouse ears

Mouse body

Origami Butterfly

Instructions
- Fold the paper in half.
- Fold the triangle in half and unfold.
- Set the triangle down with the fold pointing up, like a tent.
- Fold one corner over. Unfold.
- Fold the other corner over. Unfold.
- You have your butterfly!
- If you like, fold the butterfly in half. Cut on the dotted lines as shown to make the butterfly more rounded.

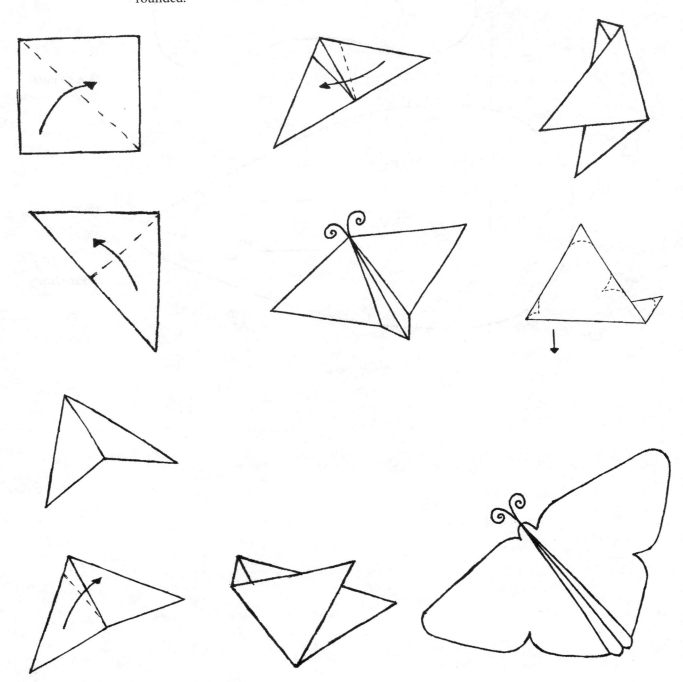

Index

Many of the ministry project ideas in chapter 2 can apply to a variety of people. For example, I See a Need is listed under the section titled People Who are Elderly, but the project is also suitable for a family shelter, a clinic or program that provides eyeglasses for people in need, or even neighbors. Similarly, kids can make lemonade not only to raise money for missions, but also to raise funds for children in need, a crisis pregnancy center, a family shelter, a food pantry, a homeless shelter, a local medical clinic, HIV/AIDS programs, medical research, a children's hospital, a soup kitchen, or even a women's shelter.

You can use the index below to help you cross-reference the multiple applications of the ministry ideas in chapter 2. As you look for ideas, don't forget that chapter 1 contains ideas that are suitable for just about anyone, and that chapter 3 contains ideas to help kids minister on holidays and special occasions.

Resource Contact Information

WMU Partnership Projects:
www.wmu.org

WorldCrafts
100 Missionary Ridge
Birmingham, AL 35242
1-800-968-7301
www.worldcraftsvillage.com

International Mission Board
P.O. Box 6767
Richmond, VA 23230-0767
1-800-999-3113
www.imb.org

North American Mission Board
4200 North Point Parkway
Alpharetta, GA 30022-4176
1-800-634-2462
www.namb.net

SBC Missions Prayer Lines:
International 1-800-395-PRAY
(www.imb.org/compassionnet/prayerline.asp)
North American 1-800-554-PRAY
(www.namb.net/prayer)

World Hunger and Relief Ministries
International Mission Board
P.O. Box 6767
Richmond, VA 23230-0767
1-800-999-3113
http://imb.org/worldhunger

Web sites for information about
people of other cultures:
www.gapassport.com
www.childrensmissions.com
www.praykids.com

Wycliffe Bible Translators
P.O. Box 628200
Orlando, FL 32862
800-WYCLIFFE
(800-992-5433)
www.wycliffe.org

World Relief
7 East Baltimore St
Baltimore MD 21202
443-451-1900 or 800-535-5433
www.wr.org

Our children visited the local food bank to help in their preparation for distribution process. When we arrived, everyone was given an orange bracelet with the food bank's name on it and we were encouraged to pray for them every time we wore the bracelet. Once inside, the children were given a large black marker and instructed to make a line through the bar code on bottles and cans of juice, water, and sport drinks. They attacked their job with enthusiasm and, in less than an hour, had marked two and a half pallets of drinks! At the end of the work session, the children were thanked and reminded that even though they will probably never get to see the people who would be receiving these drinks, they should be proud to have made a difference in a hungry and thirsty person's life. Our kids were beaming, and then said, "We're hungry!" So, they were treated to lunch. It was truly a blessing to have been a part of something much bigger than ourselves. I hope they will always remember that day. Thank you, kids and other helpers and leaders. — Ray City, Georgia

New Hope® Publishers is a division of WMU®, an international organization that challenges Christian believers to understand and be radically involved in God's mission. For more information about WMU, go to www.wmu.com. More information about New Hope books may be found at www.newhopepublishers.com. New Hope books may be purchased at your local bookstore.

More Family Fun from New Hope Publishers

Stirring Up a World of Fun
International Recipes,
Wacky Facts & Family Time Ideas
Nanette Goings
ISBN-10: 1-56309-919-5
ISBN-13: 978-1-56309-919-9

Families on Mission
Ideas for Teaching Your Preschooler
to Love, Share, and Care
Angie Quantrell
ISBN-10: 1-56309-991-8
ISBN-13: 978-1-56309-991-5

200+ Basic Faith Activities for Preschoolers
Compiled by Rhonda Reeves
ISBN-10: 1-56309-801-6
ISBN-13: 978-1-56309-801-7

Church Nanny SOS
Teaching Discipline Essentials
for Preschool Ministry Volunteers
Gigi Schweikert
ISBN-10: 1-59669-043-7
ISBN-13: 978-1-59669-043-1

New Hope
PUBLISHERS

Available in bookstores everywhere

For information about these books or any New Hope product, visit www.newhopepublishers.com.